What People are Saying About Passion For Fashion

"This book speaks of the beautiful parallel in dressing for success both in the natural and spiritual realms. I highly recommend *Passion for Fashion* to anyone who would like to grow more deeply and purely in their walk with God. Jean Metcalf uses wonderful imagery from the natural beauty and fashion world that everyone can relate to, mixed with much Scripture, to illustrate the importance of dressing and looking the part in modeling the pure, spotless bride that we are all called to be. As both a full-time revivalist and an international fashion model who stands for purity, I, for one, can relate to every ounce of the message relayed in this book and believe you will be able to as well. Whether you are a minister, model, stay-at-home mom, business owner, or student, this book is for you. After all, who doesn't want to look fashionable before the King of Kings and display his great glory on the Earth?"

— Miranda Nelson

Professional Fashion Model and Cofounder, Elisha Revolution

"There is a French idiom that has an approximate equivalent in English: 'To feel good about yourself.' In more than forty years of full-time ministry, I have discovered that vast multitudes of people don't feel good about themselves—including many Christians. The incessant lies of the adversary and the pressures of popular culture conspire to cause them to feel inferior, unworthy, and unloved.

"Jean Metcalf knows what it is like to experience these feelings—but she also knows what it takes to overcome them. She has learned how to prevail over rejection, depression, and bitterness, and today is an example of elegance, poise, and grace.

"Her examples will inspire anyone who has ever struggled with issues of unworthiness or inferiority to experience the vibrant and victorious life that our Lord Jesus Christ provided through His death, burial, and resurrection from the grave. That same power is available to you today, and Jean does a masterful job of helping you achieve God's grand design for your life."

— **Dr. Rod Parsley**
Pastor and Founder, World Harvest Church
Columbus, Ohio

"I have had the opportunity to serve Jean and her husband, Greg, as their pastor for many years. In all the time I have known them, their faithfulness and energy for the Lord and His purposes have never diminished. The title of her new book, *Passion for Fashion*, is appropriate. Jean's heart desire is to see God's people be passionate about living out their part in God's plan.

"Jean is, among other good things, passionate herself—passionate about her family, passionate about helping people, and passionate about taking the Gospel to the whole world. She has been steady through trials, faithful to God's house, and generous with her time and resources. I know that the wisdom she has gained through years in the Word, and through experiencing God's faithfulness in the good times and the hard times, will be of great benefit to you.

"The metaphors and examples she uses in her book, *Passion for Fashion*, will definitely 'hit the bulls eye' with many people. She shares eternal truths in a fresh way. Enjoy and learn."

— Bayless Conley
Senior Pastor, Cottonwood Church
Los Alamitos, California

"In a very unique and creative way, Jean Metcalf presents biblical truths that will help you walk in the freedom that God intended for you. Her honesty is refreshing, and her approach is practical. This work is truthful, humorous, and liberating."

— David Diga Hernandez
Author and Evangelist

"*Passion for Fashion* by Jean Metcalf is a beautiful book written expressly for women that will be a great source of wisdom and help to all women. It contains many Scriptures with practical advice on how to walk out the call of God in your life. I know you will benefit from reading and applying the truths in this book."

— Joan Hunter

Author and Evangelist

"I highly recommend this amazing book. With a fourteen-year retail background, I have truly enjoyed every page of this book. I have had the privilege and honor to know Jean personally and have observed her great taste in fashion. I believe that as you read this book, you will see Jean's love for Jesus in her walk and her commitment to fulfilling the call God is giving her. What touches my heart as I read this book is to see that her love is so transparent. Get ready to go into transition because you will hear the heart of the Father giving you identity and a clear look at how He sees you. Be ready to be transformed to His fashion. I feel that this book is so needed in this generation. As women, we were created to show the beauty in which God created us. I have never read a book about fashion that displays heaven so well."

— Silvia Sanford

Realtor® and Founder, Silvia Sanford Ministries, Raising Deborahs

"Jean Metcalf exemplifies the highest example of what it means to be a Christian. She literally models the life of the supernatural believer by putting into practice the very principles she shares in this powerful book. In this current culture, it is paramount that every believer learns how to remove the artificial facades the challenges of life often pressure us to wear. These masks are often the undetected barrier to experiencing the fullest level of victorious power that God desires for us. In this masterful writing, you will learn how to break free from the bondages of your past, and with an emphatic passion, become the confident and supernatural person God made you! This book is a must-read for every believer!"

— Pastors Hank and Brenda Kunneman
Lord of Hosts Church and One Voice Ministries
Omaha, Nebraska

"Jean Metcalf, my dear friend, has shared both her heart and her passion with us in her book, *Passion for Fashion*. Over all the years that I have known Jean, her passion and first love have always been the power and the presence of God. Her heart's desire is to be clothed in righteousness. She definitely has a passion for fashion in the natural and spirit realms.

"In *Passion for Fashion*, Jean shares her own testimony and practical steps on how she overcame painful, heartbreaking life experiences and reached for God's supernatural strength and healing power to stand in the place of victory and wholeness.

"I believe each reader will be able to identify with the steps to healing and wholeness outlined in Jean's book. And you will be challenged to press on to the higher calling in Christ Jesus. When you allow Jesus to shatter your shame and you say, 'Be gone!' to your guilt, you will be released to the next level. In doing so, you will be ready to walk the runway of God's design for your life!"

— **Rev. Danette J. Crawford**
Founder and President, Danette Crawford Ministries
Virginia Beach, Virginia

"Jean Metcalf is a force to be reckoned with! A leader in business with a heart for the Kingdom, her new book, *Passion for Fashion*, shares her moving testimony, along with life-changing insights. The contrasts Jean draws between fashion and being a godly woman is a read that everyone will love. Don't miss out on this powerful book!"

— **Pastor Dan Willis**
Senior Pastor, Lighthouse Church of All Nations
Chicago, Illinois

"Jean Metcalf provides the reader with the ultimate template to uncovering biblical principles in a road-map format that anyone can follow to unlock their fullest potential in life. She is a biblical mentor-in-print who systematically addresses key challenging areas in life and breaks them down into simple steps that anyone who reads this faith-building treasure of hope can implement right away. There are so many gems of wisdom in this easy-to-read book that you will find yourself reading it over and over again!"

— Kimberly Cravotta-Purvis, MS, LMFT
Clinical Therapist

"Passion for Fashion is a book that speaks to the soul and heart. It is a book of clear scriptural and Holy Spirit-filled instruction. If your heart's desire is to be like Jesus, this is a book for you. You may have some struggles and disappointments in your life, but your heart is fixed. You are ready for this book."

"Through the power of the Holy Spirit and the love of God, this book is written in total transparency to reach out to you, touch you, and give you hope and the presence of God. Jesus said it this way: 'My peace I give unto you, not as the world gives, give I unto you, let not your heart be troubled neither let it be afraid.'"

"This book, through Divine inspiration, will take you from the defense to the offense. It will be one of God's tools for His Divine intervention and victory in your life. It will encourage your heart so that you have blessed full assurance that if God be for you, who can be against you? It will fill your heart with Divine anticipation that something good is going to happen to you. You will know in your heart that Jesus is the same yesterday, today, and forever and that the blueprint of your life is full of miracles. As you hold this book, Jesus is passing your way."

— **Jerry Moses**
Assistant to the President, Movieguide®

"When I read your book, my conviction became alive in your story: that when a believer is squeezed, the beautiful, passionate aroma comes out. This unique story, coming from a unique woman like you, represents hope, beauty, and elegance."

— **Yvette Isaac**
General Director, Roads of Success Team
Duarte, California

PASSION
for Fashion

WALKING THE RUNWAY OF *GOD'S* DESIGN

JEAN METCALF
FOREWORD by DR. MARILYN HICKEY

I dedicate this book to Mom and Dad, who gave me a passion for life and introduced me to fashion modeling. They taught me how to walk with my eyes focused forward on God, His Word, and His plan for my life. They instructed me to love the Lord Jesus with all my heart, soul, and body. They coached me to trust Him and not depend on my own ways of thinking. This book is a continuation of their legacy.

Published by HigherLife Development Services, Inc.
PO Box 623307
Oviedo, Florida 32762
(407) 563-4806
www.ahigherlife.com

ISBN #978-1-7328859-1-2
ISBN # 978-1-7328859-2-9

First Edition
13 14 15 16 17 —12 11 10 9 8 7 6 5

Printed in Canada

WALKING THE RUNWAY OF GOD'S DESIGN

FOREWORD

The book *Passion for Fashion* is very important, I believe, to every woman because in some way, we are all born with a desire to be fashionable. Even most men desire to look clean and presentable. When my granddaughter, Isabel, was born, life changed for my daughter, Sarah, who is more tomboyish and more athletic. Wouldn't you know, God gave her a girly-girl—Isabel loves fashion. She said to me one day, "Maybe you will have some jewelry you would like to pass on to me because you and I are alike!"

Too cute! Even so, Sarah likes fashion for her way of life, her way of thinking. This book, *Passion for Fashion,* will help you see that God has a plan for the role of fashion in this life. He puts in you the image to be the model He desires for you so that you can walk out your life while on Earth.

Jean Metcalf has been a very good friend to me for some years. I know her, her husband Greg, and their sons. It has been a great privilege to have the opportunity to personally mentor Jean. I see that her heart is so pure and so directed to what God wants in every level of her life. I appreciate this book because I know the author very well. I know the passion and the purity of her heart to walk in God's anointing and righteousness. But I also know how much she wants to pass it on. It is Jean's desire to mentor you through her books. She is passing on to you her insight about how to walk in the Word and how to be dressed for success. Will you receive that mantle of *Passion for Fashion—Walking the Runway of God's Design*?

— **Dr. Marilyn Hickey**

Founder and President

Marilyn Hickey Ministries

INTRODUCTION

"Jesus said, so love the Lord your God with
all your passion and prayer
and intelligence and energy."
Mark 12:30 (MSG)

A fashion show is a fun place to be—as a designer, a photographer, a choreographer, a model, or in the audience. The atmosphere is intense with expectation for the new season's designs. Everyone is running around handling last-minute details. The crowd buzzes with anticipation.

I was introduced to fashion by my mother, who signed me up for etiquette school with Florence Smales Modeling Agency. I was thirteen years old when I did a photo shoot for my portfolio. The photographer said I took good pictures but that I should get my teeth straightened for a more refined look. By the time I got my teeth done, I was in high school and didn't want to pursue modeling. However, fashion has been a part of my life since that time.

At age fifteen, I got involved in a youth group and started reading the Bible. The more I read it, the hungrier for God I became. Later on, I did a Word study about walking in the Word, the Bible. There is a lot of Scripture that instructs us on how to walk out our lives. Walk in love. Walk worthy of our calling. Walk by faith, not by sight. Walk in wisdom, etc.

One day, years later, I was imagining walking on a fashion runway. Then I thought about God being my Designer and walking His runway for my life. Often, what is in the natural world can be related to what's happening in the supernatural world.

My mind continued to put the two ways of walking together, and *Passion for Fashion* was born. The expectation of a fashion show continued to illuminate my thinking when I attended a large gathering of people assembled to worship and be in the presence of the Holy Spirit. That same excitement of anticipation was there in a healing crusade.

The Designer is God. Jesus is the Designer's Son in charge of the garment industry. He is the One who clothes you with robes of righ-

---

We are the models who walk God's runway of life.

---

teousness. The photographer is the one who takes pictures to remember the event. The choreographer is the Holy Spirit, who orchestrates the meeting. We are the models who walk God's runway of life. The audience is composed of those watching.

After the praise, worship, and message, people who have been healed, or are in the process of healing, tell their stories of how Jesus touched their bodies. I am amazed when I see the look on the faces of people who came filled with back pain and no longer have it. Others, who have had lumps in various places in their bodies, come up to show that the lump is gone.

Praise erupts to God from the crowd, building momentum for more of the Holy Spirit's presence. That is the environment in which faith and passion have an opportunity to explode.

The word *passion* means "boundless enthusiasm." The word *enthusiasm* comes from the Greek words *en*, meaning "in," and *theo*, meaning "God."

When you are passionate about your purpose, and when your desire is to see God's handiwork in your life, you are "in God" and overflowing with exuberant excitement. That's why I am so excited that you are reading this book. Today, many distractions pull at us at all times. We have a choice about what we dwell on, look at, and enjoy.

My desire is that as you read this book, you will be encouraged in who you are in God's eyes. Dress for success, and be confident in the way you walk through life. Be full of enthusiasm about growing in the knowledge of the Word of God. I want you to hunger for an intimate relationship with the Holy Spirit. When you have experienced the presence of Holy Spirit in your life, you will never be the same. This book is based on the Word of God and its promises. If you live by the concepts on these pages, your life will be divinely transformed. You will have that "knowing" of who Jesus is in your life and understand how to make it all come together.

Here are four ways this book can help you grow in your faith:

1. You will take off the wrong clothes. You will discover that breaking away from bondage is possible.

2. You will learn how to walk by faith, not by what you see.

3. You will understand the spiritual authority that has been given to you through your relationship with Jesus Christ. You will have authority when you speak the Word and God's promises over a particular situation.

4. You will find out that there are many, many voices out there and learn to discern the right one to listen to.

Knowing these points, you will be fully equipped to lead a life full of passion for your purpose.

I'm excited for your journey. Get ready to live with passion for Jesus, and allow the Holy Spirit to fashion you into the likeness of His Glory.

CHAPTER 1
Remove the Wrong Clothing

The night is almost gone; the day of
salvation will soon be here. So remove your
dark deeds like dirty clothes...
Romans 13:12 (NLT)

Have you ever gotten dressed and not felt right about your outfit? I have. Sometimes I go through more than one ensemble before being comfortable with the clothing. The outfit has to be appropriate for the occasion. It has to fit well—not too tight, not too loose. The color must be well-suited to you as well. You feel good about yourself when you wear clothes you like that also look good on you.

Both in your everyday life and in your walk of faith, take off the wrong clothes. Remove what you have been covered with. Get rid of the defiant attitude. Strip away the hate, bitterness, and immoral behavior. Cast off the drugs, alcohol, and porn. Instead, be fashionable in God's eyes, and be a reflection of the inner beauty He has given you. You were created in His image, but because of the fall of Adam and Eve, you have to deal with that broken relationship. Jesus came to Earth to be the bridge between our holy God and sinful man. The New Living Translation says in Isaiah 64:6, "We are all infected and impure with sin. When we display our righteous deeds, they are nothing but *filthy rags*." Our clothes in the natural world are not filthy rags, but you get the idea.

REPENT TO REMOVE THE WRONG SPIRITUAL CLOTHING

You know how to take off your clothes in the natural world, but how do you do that in the supernatural world? To *take off* means "to disrobe or strip." Move beyond your past—the dirt that covers the real you. Disrobe from all the layers of pain, disappointment, and emotional hurt you have experienced in your life. Take off the wrong clothing.

This starts with repentance. Turn away from the past, which is saying you are sorry for everything you have done wrong. You desire to sin

---

Have a conversation with the One who fashioned you.

---

no longer. You are sorry for putting yourself first. You admit to God that you can't live this life on your own. Put Jesus on the throne of your life. Declare that Jesus is Lord. Saying this and meaning it is a vocal sign that you are aligning yourself with God's design. Pray, which is talking with God. Have a conversation with the One who fashioned you. He hears you and will listen to your prayers.

Then give Jesus all your distress, discomfort, and disappointments. You no longer have to carry the world on your shoulders. Usually that doesn't happen overnight. It has taken me years to remove insecurity, disappointments, and regrets. The closer I get to God, the more I read His Word, and the more my trust in the Holy Spirit grows. When I do this, layers of pain are lifted from me. Today, when I think about a situation that caused hidden hurt, those feelings of rejection don't well up inside me anymore.

Trusting God is well worth it. Today, I have much more freedom than I have ever had. I am comfortable with who I am and who I have become. Do I have more layers that need to be removed? Of course I do, and I have asked God for help in this area. As He continues to help me follow His will, I can enjoy my life because I have put Jesus in control.

Change is a part of life. Transformation is a 180-degree turnaround from the way you used to think, a reprogramming of your mind to a new perspective. Matthew 3:1–2 says in the Passion translation, "The realm of heaven's kingdom is about to appear—so you'd better keep turning away from evil and turn back to God." Other translations use the word "repent."

The word "repent" in Greek is *metanoeo* (G-3340), which means "to think differently; to change one's mind and purpose as the result of after knowledge." Also, "repent" means "feeling regretful for past conduct and to turn away from sin." When you repent, darkness no longer surrounds you. Instead, forgiveness will flood you with light. Sometimes it's hardest to forgive yourself.

> *Now Joshua (the high priest) had on filthy garments and was standing before the angel. And he (the angel) said to those standing before him, "Take off his filthy garments." Then he said, "See that I have removed from you your iniquity, and I will clothe you with rich robes."*
> —Zechariah 3:3-4 (MEV)

This is an illustration in which the high priest, Joshua, was standing in the Courts of Heaven. He had sinned and was wearing dirty clothes. Satan was accusing the judge of his sin. But God knew the heart of Joshua. In verse 2, the LORD said to Satan, "The LORD rebuke you, Satan!"

The word "LORD" in capital letters in the Old Testament implies that He is the eternal Father of relationship and covenant.

Learn to walk through heaven's gates with thanksgiving and into His courts with praise (Ps. 100:4). When you pray to God, approach Him first with thanksgiving for all He has done for you. Then praise God, giving glory for who He is (faithful, forgiving, righteous, majestic, and full of honor). When the devil is accusing you, have Scriptures to remind yourself of God, the Judge, and of His Word. Be ready to show the Court why you are to be given an innocent verdict. The Blood of the Lamb has redeemed you. You have accepted the forgiveness given to you at the cross. Take off your unclean apparel. Let Jesus Christ be the Mediator, the advocate He was designed to be. Let Him cover you with a wonderful wardrobe.

> *I am overwhelmed with joy in the LORD my God! For He*
> *has dressed me with the clothing of salvation and draped*
> *me in a robe of righteousness.*
> —Isaiah 61:10 (NLT)

Tell Jesus you are sorry for dwelling on the hurt and pain in your life. Take control of your thought process. Put your spirit in control, not your feelings.

It is not wrong to experience sorrow and misery. But your mind has a tendency to go over the hurtful events day after day. Continuously thinking about the wounds can cause evil spirits of pity and grief to enter your soul and become all-absorbing. That's when you need to talk with Jesus and tell Him how sorry you are for constantly consuming wrong thoughts.

Were you wounded? Well, yes, but you need to forgive and forget.

Only Jesus can make you well. He is Jehovah Rapha, God our healer. He is God our health. Let Jesus heal you by taking off the soiled garments that have covered you. Let Him dress you with His fashion, His likeness, His glory.

I have had to remind myself to do that on several occasions. I am a sensitive person. I am a nurturer. I am empathetic and feel emotional hurt—not only mine, but others' as well. This usually relates to family or friends; those we are closest to often disappoint us the most. Many times, people have misunderstood what I said or how I said it. I have endured incessant yelling. At times, my legs would get weak and tremble.

I don't like conflict. I realize now what was going on. The person was not attacking me; Satan was influencing my family member. So I immediately forgave the person.

I encourage you to realize what is happening and forgive the person who is in conflict with you. When those thoughts of resentment come back to you, hold them up to Jesus and say, "I am giving those thoughts and feelings to You. I don't want to hold on to them anymore. You wore the crown of thorns so I could wear the crown of righteousness. I don't have to deal with the pain and the thorny thoughts any longer. Thank You for loving me so much."

Remember, the battlefield is in the mind. When those feelings of heartache come back again, say, "Oh, no, you don't, devil. I gave those feelings to Jesus. He is dealing with them, not me. Now, go."

I first got married when I was twenty-two. I thought I was in love with a man who loved me and that life would be wonderful. I dreamed we would have three children and live in a ranch-style home with French windows.

When I told my mom that we were engaged to be married, she told me without hesitation, "You don't know what love is."

I was offended and was determined to prove her wrong. But after eight years of marriage my husband left our adopted son and me. We had grown apart, having never spent time together.

Earlier he had told me, "I don't love you the way you love me."

I thought, "God, what does that mean?"

I remember late nights when I could not go to sleep because my husband was not home yet. I would get up, put my robe on, sit in the living room on the big sofa, and pray in the dark.

Being a limo driver, he would often arrive home after 2 a.m. He'd come through the front door and go to the bedroom, never realizing I was watching him.

After many days, he called me while I was at work and said, "Let's go to your mom's house for dinner tonight. I've asked her to make a meal for us. You have been working so hard, you need a break."

I thought, "Really? Are you kidding me? Maybe he has changed."

Then he said, "Let's take two cars in case I get called to work." Sure enough, he got a call to do a job. Later, when we got home, I put my son to bed and walked into the master bedroom. I stopped. The chest of drawers was gone. I thought we had been robbed. Then I saw a letter on my side of the bed.

Life is not always what you think it's going to be. My husband had abandoned me, both emotionally and physically. Divorce had never crossed my mind. After all, I was a Christian, and our wedding vows said, "until death do us part." Covenants can be broken. It takes two people to make a marriage.

We have a choice to put off, take off, and get rid of the old way of thinking. Remove the wrong clothes. Healing is a process. Welcome a new mindset. First, make a decision to change. Then say aloud a verse from the Bible pertaining to your circumstances.

My verse for that situation was Jeremiah 29:11 (NIV), "'For I know the plans that I have for you', declares the LORD, 'plans to prosper you and not to harm you, plans to give you hope and a future.'" I wrote that on a 3x5 card and put it on the refrigerator.

We must realize that our words are important. The book of Genesis talks about God creating the universe with His words. Genesis 1:3 says, "Then God said, 'Let there be light'; and there was light."

We are created in His image, His fashion, and we create and fashion our world with our words. The atmosphere you bring about all starts

---

The words you speak formulate your world.

---

with your thoughts. Then your thoughts become your words. Instead of just reading, speak out loud those Bible verses you have on your refrigerator, mirror, or cell phone. Remember, the words you speak formulate your world.

FOUR TYPES OF SPEAKING TO REMOVE FROM OUR LIVES

There are at least four areas that have to do with your words that you must put off and get rid of if you want to be fashioned in the image of God.

> *But now you yourselves are to **put off** all these: Anger, wrath, malice, blasphemy, filthy language out of your mouth. Do not lie to one another since you have **put off** the old man with his deeds, and have **put on** the new man who is renewed in knowledge according to the **image** of Him who created him" [emphasis mine here and in all other Bible citations in the book where some words appear in bold].*
>
> —Colossians 3:8–10

1. **Lying**—"Don't lie to one another." Lying creates division and a lack of trust. If you have messed up, just tell me, but don't lie to me. My first husband was a chronic liar. I was always taught to think the best of someone. Believe he is telling the truth. Well, I learned that is not always the case.

2. **Gossiping and back biting**—Proverbs 16:28 says, "A whisperer separates the best of friends." Hearsay is common. Look at the number of gossip magazines, TV shows, and internet stories. Slander and backbiting are abundant, just the way the devil likes it.

3. **Complaining**—Complaining is otherwise known as *murmuring*. When you murmur, you get a crack in the hedge of safety that surrounds you. As Christians, we live under God's protection, His umbrella. But it is dangerous territory if you continue to complain. Complaining creates a crack in the wall of protection surrounding you. That opening will let evil in. Numbers 12:1 says, "Complaining is a form of rebellion." And 1 Samuel 15:23 (KJV) says, "Rebellion is as the sin of witchcraft."

4. **Excessive talking**—Proverbs 17:27 says, "A person with knowledge will restrain his tongue." Proverbs 10:19 says, in the Passion translation, "If you keep talking, it won't be long before you're saying something really wrong. Prove you're wise from the very start—just bite your tongue and be strong!" I know people who talk a lot. They want to tell you every detail. Usually it's women who talk. But men can talk a lot as well. Zip the lip. When you've said enough, stop.

Of these four negative points related to communication, my weakness used to be complaining: "Why did this happen to me? I didn't do anything wrong. I didn't deserve this." Sure, I still complain, like when there is too much traffic, which is often in southern California where I live.

I used to complain about not liking certain kinds of food or the weather. "It's too cold" or "It's too hot." Sometimes I'm still like the fairy tale of the Princess and the Pea, who likes everything just so. I have a five-degree comfort level. OK, maybe ten degrees.

I'm working on always saying positive things and avoiding the tendency to murmur. I have so many things to be thankful for. We all do.

Be thankful for what you have, the many blessings you have been given. Have an attitude of gratitude. Have a thankful heart. Spending time in the presence of the Lord will make you appreciative. Worship Jesus, and let the Holy Spirit talk to you. He will show you in the Bible the great things Jesus has done for you. Doing this will heal your heart. Thanksgiving will flow from your innermost being through your voice in praise. The wrong will be removed.

CHAPTER 2
Cleansed in the Spa of Heaven

"Cleanse me with hyssop, and I will be
clean; Wash me, and I will be whiter
than snow."
Psalm 51:7 (NIV)

After you discard the old clothes and get rid of your past mindset, it's time to be cleansed. Do you like to go to the spa? I do. I don't get to go very often, but when the plan is in place, I look forward to the amazing day with anticipation. A spa day is a time to rejuvenate, relax, and restore your body. Fountains of flowing waters surround you like living

---

You can have a spa day at home.

---

water that flows from the Throne of God to restore your soul.

You don't have to go to a spa; you can have a spa day at home.

First comes a facial. Cleansing the skin with a hydrating cleanser is the best way to begin. Take the second, third, and fourth fingers of each hand, and use a circular motion to penetrate the outer layers of the skin. The following procedure is to exfoliate, the process of washing with a granular cosmetic preparation with serum or lotion to remove dead cells from the skin surface.

Exfoliate the whole body in your bathtub at least once a month.

When you are in the presence of the Lord, the dead cells get taken off your life. Hosea 10:12 (NIV) says, "Sow for yourselves righteousness, reap the fruit of unfailing love; and break up your unplowed ground; for it is time to seek the LORD…"

Breaking up hard dirt may be a little far-fetched, but it's a hard heart or hard ground that keeps us from absorbing the Word of God. The point is to exfoliate your soul so you can have a clean heart.

> *That He might sanctify and cleanse it with the washing*
> *of the water by the Word, that He might present it to*
> *Himself a glorious church, not having spot or wrinkle,*
> *or any such thing; But that it should be holy and without*
> *blemish.*
> —Ephesians 5:26–27 (KJV)

Exfoliation is rejuvenation. It takes only a few days for the skin cells to build up again. Daily gentle exfoliation will remove the worldly attitudes and wrong words that have been said. Replace these disappointments with reading and speaking God's promises. Raise your hands, and close your eyes, and worship Jesus.

Next, place a warm, moist towel on your face. This opens the pores of the skin to receive the nutrients of the mask. This product is usually made of clay.

Spiritually speaking, "Your youth is renewed like the eagle's" (Ps. 103:5). Your spirit, soul, and body are refreshed when you spend time in the presence of the Holy Spirit.

When the facial is complete, a body massage can follow. Therapeutic kneading of the muscles by a trained professional relaxes the tenseness in your muscles. Toxins are released as well, so drink lots of water afterward.

Now sink into a spa tub with extra-warm, bubbly water to further loosen the knots in your muscles. Relaxing will calm your mind as well.

When you have been set free of lying, gossiping, and complaining, your mind can relax. You will no longer have to remember the lies you said or whom you gossiped to and what about. When your mind unwinds, your body will follow suit.

> *He [Jesus] rose and rebuked the wind, and said to the*
> *sea, "Peace be still!" Then the wind ceased and there*
> *was a great **calm.***
> —Mark 4:39

Continued relaxation happens in the sauna, where hot, moist heat cleanses even deeper into the skin to remove more toxins. Lying, gossip, and complaining are toxins. Breathe deep; exhale slowly through your mouth. Let go of the stress in your life. Let go of the day's distractions. Focus on being in the Spa of Heaven. Be renewed and revived.

QUEEN ESTHER WAS CLEANSED IN THE SPA OF HEAVEN

Queen Esther in the Old Testament prepared herself for a year before she entered the King's presence for the first time. (See Esther 2:12–16.) She indulged in lots of emollient creams, body lotions, pedicures, manicures, and facials. She spent the first six months of treatment using oil of myrrh to soften and condition her skin and make it smooth and supple.

Fragrant myrrh stirs love. Esther soaked herself daily in love.

When you take time daily to read the Word of God, speak the promises, pray, and worship; you are soaking yourself in God's love. He *is*

Let Jesus Christ carry your burdens.

---

love. (See 1 John 4:16.) When you realize how much your Abba Father loves you, you will feel content and peaceful. You will know the Father is taking care of you.

We do not have to carry the world on our shoulders. We were not made to do that. Let Jesus Christ carry your burdens, your sorrows, and your grief. He did this for us on the cross. He also took on our worries, anxieties, and pains, both physically and emotionally.

A humble and thankful heart will allow you to get on your knees at the foot of the cross. Immerse yourself in the hot tub of the presence of the Holy Spirit. Worshipping Jesus allows your spirit to soak in His glory. Having a tender spirit makes it easy to receive His love.

In natural warm water, oils will penetrate your skin, making it soft and supple. In my study at home, I enjoy putting praise and worship music on and walking around the room, praying in my heavenly language, speaking God's promises to back up what I am praying for in the natural world. I speak many Bible verses out loud each day to renew my spirit.

Soaking in God's presence allows the oil of the Holy Spirit to make your heart soft. It took me a long time to get to this place, but now I cannot live without spending time in the Spa of Heaven.

Take a long hard look. See how great He is—infinite, greater than anything you could ever imagine or figure out! He pulls water up out of the sea, distills it, and fills up His cisterns. Then the skies open up and pour our soaking showers on everyone.
—Job 36:26-27 (MSG)

Be cleansed, and purify your heart. No more affliction, pain, or worry. You no longer have to keep it and deal with it alone. When Jesus died, He said, "It is finished." The final verdict was spoken.

What do you have to worry about? You can't do anything about that stuff anyway, right? Let go, and let Jesus have it. He will work it out beyond what we could ask or imagine.

Jesus did all this so you could live free from pain. He didn't want you to feel pressed down, shoved under, and pushed back. Instead, it is His desire for you to be full of joy as the Bride of Christ. A bride prepares herself for the amazing day when she will be married to the man she loves. Her happiness and joy will be over the top. That is how Jesus Christ wants you to live your life every day.

Just as a bride is immersed in her husband's love, Jesus loves for us to be immersed in that spa of His love, His presence. His desire is for you to allow the Word of God to penetrate your spirit and allow it to be ready to receive a fresh revelation of who He is.

Let us draw near with a true heart in full assurance of faith, having our hearts sprinkled from an evil conscience and our bodies washed with pure water.
—Hebrews 10:22 (NKJV)

CLEANSE YOUR SPIRIT THROUGH THE WORD OF GOD

Supernaturally speaking, you are cleansed and revived through the Word of God. Read the Word. Memorize the Word. Speak the Word. The Bible is the foundation of who you are. That is the belt of Truth. Jesus is Truth. He said in John 14:6, "I am the way, the TRUTH and the Life…"

When you memorize God's Word, you have His promises hidden in your heart so that when you need them, they come up out of your spirit so you can speak them. It's like that double-edged sword in Ephesians 6:17 that says, "The sword of the Spirit, which is the Word of God." It's that spoken Word of God that goes into your heart and comes out your mouth. That is where true God-power comes from.

Speaking the promises of God from the Bible is what you need while you are on Earth. When you are in prayer, imagine being in the Courts of Heaven. The devil is the accuser, and Jesus is the Mediator. Present your case to the Judge (God) with evidence from Scripture. How do we know there is a court in heaven? Daniel 7 talks about Daniel having night visions and seeing into the Courts of Heaven.

> *I watched till thrones were put in place, and the Ancient of Days was seated; His garment was white as snow, and the hair of His head was like pure wool. His throne as a fiery flame, its wheels burning fire; a fiery stream issued and came forth from before Him. A thousand thousands ministered to Him; ten thousand times ten thousand stood before Him. The **court** was seated, and the books were opened.*
>
> ----Daniel 7:9-10 (NKJV)

You and I must learn to execute the verdict by speaking out about the promises from the Bible in every situation. This is done in the Courts of Heaven. It is written in Galatians 3:13 that Christ has redeemed us from the curse of the law. That is a verdict reiterated by the apostle Paul. When we speak out that verse, we are declaring evidence that we have been given that verdict, which is executed when we declare the promises of God. Praising God and shouting in the Courts of Heaven is how we make our petitions. This is where we pray for ourselves and others. This is where victory is ensured.

When I am done speaking the promises of the Bible and praising God, I will sit and get quiet before the Lord so I can listen to the Holy Spirit. I'll worship and/or sing quietly or just be silent. I call that entering the Holy Place. Total resilience happens in that place.

The Holy of Holies is a place of complete awe and reverence. This is a position in the Holy Spirit that results when you have been worshipping and meditating on God's Word. You no longer give your prayer requests; you are there to just listen and enjoy the presence of Jesus. I am unable to go there often because I get distracted with thoughts about what needs to be done that day. Sometimes it is hard to be quiet. But my desire is to be there.

I most definitely want to be more of a Mary than a Martha. Luke 10 mentions two sisters who dearly loved Jesus while He walked on Earth. Martha was a server and very practical about presenting her home and food for the special occasion. In contrast, her sister, Mary, would sit at the feet of Jesus while He taught the Word of God. She didn't want to be bothered with everyday issues. Of course, we need both Mary- and Martha-type ambitions in our lives.

The Spa of Heaven is a place in God's Presence to prepare you for the journey He has designed for you. Preparation can take a long time. I can't imagine going to a spa every day for a year, as Queen Esther did. She prepared herself to meet the king. Look what she accomplished because she was led by the Holy Spirit, even though she didn't realize it. The Jewish people were saved from extinction. Because of Queen Esther's obedience, Jesus the Messiah would eventually be born of Jewish heritage.

When we obey the voice of the Holy Spirit and worship Him, our books in heaven are opened. Those books have our names on them. Our destiny, written in those books, is revealed. Don't look back and be discouraged because you haven't yet reached your goals and dreams. Your time has not been wasted.

Your timing is not God's timing.

Everything you have gone through, whether good or bad, is meant to make you the person God designed you to be for His honor and glory. Your timing is not God's timing. Isaiah 55:8 tells us, "'For My thoughts are not your thoughts, nor are your ways my ways,' says the LORD."

You don't always understand, but don't doubt.

> *Trust in the LORD completely, and do not rely on your*
> *own opinions. With all your heart rely on him to guide*
> *you, and he will lead you in every decision you make.*
> —Proverbs 3:5-6 (TPT)

CHANGE TAKES TIME

In 2003, I took a Bible study course called "Never-Ending Word Studies" by Dr. Mary Giangreco. I learned during this two-year program how to study the Word of God and why it is important to be a serious student. I learned to journal. I still write down the thoughts and God-inspired ideas that come to my mind.

We discussed how to do a Word study, an itemized study, a character study, and an essay study.

When I got into it, I couldn't get enough of the Word. I learned how to use *Strong's Concordance* to look up the Hebrew or Greek version of Scriptures and delve into the meaning of the words. I graduated after completing an essay study on the book of Amos.

I chose Amos because he was a minor prophet in the Old Testament, and it was a short book. But I discovered that there was much more in that book than I realized.

After graduating, I thought I was ready to be a speaker, write a book, travel the world sharing the love of Jesus Christ, and more. But that was a long time ago. Time and preparation—and, oh yes, life—got in the way. Maybe I was ready in a lot of ways to be a speaker, and I did some speaking, but I needed internal healing from bitterness and disappointments. I needed to grow up.

Never give up on your dreams. You are not wasting your time.

Change usually does not happen in an instant. Often in this day of fast food, convenience stores, and same-day shipping, you get what you want quickly. But when it comes to job promotions, growing in faith, and emotional or physical healing, the process usually takes more time than we wish it would.

Do what you need to do in the natural world to attain the goals you have set. A job advancement takes increased skills and a spirit of excellence. Preparing to be a fashion model requires much practice and preparation before a fashion show.

I encourage you to cleanse yourself in the Spa of Heaven daily as you prepare for the runway of your life. Just like Esther prepared herself to meet the king by cleansing her body in the spa, cleanse daily in God's spa to be prepared to live according to God's purpose. Cleansing your spirit, soul, and body prepares you for promotion.

CHAPTER 3
From Bondage to Breakthrough

For you did not receive the spirit of
bondage again to fear, but you received
the Spirit of adoption by whom we cry out,
"Abba, Father."
Romans 8:14–15 (NKJV)

To walk the runway of life with courage and confidence, whether in the fashion industry or in our daily lives, we must break free from bondage or attachment to things that separate us from our walk with God. Having a breakthrough is a process, much like preparation is a process. When you need a breakthrough, it's because bondage has you stuck.

God has fashioned us to walk with power, love, and sound minds. In 2 Timothy 1:7, we are reminded that we have not been given a spirit of fear. Timidity keeps us from walking tall with one foot in front of the other. Apprehension can make our shoulders droop and dim the sparkle in our eyes. That is why it is important to learn to walk in freedom.

I believe the spirit of bondage is the easiest, most deceptive demonic weapon out there. Usually, being confined in this way doesn't grab you overnight. Instead, entrapment will slowly slither around you like a snake, the spirit of a python attempting to squeeze the life out of you. Bondage will keep you from wanting to step out of your comfort zone and do what God has called for you to do for His Kingdom.

EMOTIONAL BONDAGE OFTEN BEGINS IN CHILDHOOD

Emotional slavery comes in many types and degrees. You can be constrained for many reasons. Those things that keep you imprisoned are physical, emotional, or both. You might have insecurities that stem from the pain of rejection or abandonment. Most often, emotional bondage starts in childhood, when your parents have the greatest power and influence over you. Generally, they do what they know to do, and they probably did the best they could to raise you. But sadly, in many cases,

---

Insecurities come from rejection.

---

children are ignored, abandoned, or abused. If you have experienced these devastating circumstances, my heart goes out to you.

Feelings of rejection and abandonment can be intense. Rejection can take the form of being bullied by other kids to your parents getting a divorce. Whether rejection is real or only perceived, the emotional damage is the same.

Abandonment is either physical or emotional. Physical abandonment is when a parent permanently moves out of the home. Emotional abandonment is when loved ones are not there for you when you are hurting. They might not be there for you when you are happy, either. The result is insecurity and a feeling of being inadequate.

That was me. I experienced emotional bondage. My father was a doctor who was always at the emergency room or the office. He would come home late at night when I was already in bed. In the morning, I was up and off to school and didn't see him then, either.

Often, when we're young, we don't realize what we're missing. We just do what we've always done and accept an absent father or mother as normal. My dad was a wonderful Christian who loved and provided for the family, but he didn't know how to relate to his children. I didn't get to know my dad until I was sixteen and took a biology class. We would study science together. He helped me with that subject because he knew it so well. We laughed together and bonded as father and daughter. (And yes, I received an "A" in that class.)

A decade later, while married to my first husband, I worked in my dad's medical practice doing office work. I had previously worked in another doctor's office, so I knew what to do. Dad trained me to handle the tasks that needed to be done in his practice.

My dad and I had a great working relationship. Finally, I was able to get to know and understand him. He taught me the medical protocol for the office and how to read a cervical and lumbar MRI. Then he would ask me to read another patient's MRI, diagnose the patient's condition, and tell him why I came to that conclusion. He said I was smart and that I could be a neurosurgeon if I wanted. I looked forward to our chatting and bonding together. I always referred to him as "Doctor" in the office. I did it so much that when we were in a family situation, I still referred to him as "Doctor" instead of "Dad."

I was fortunate. But many are not.

What's worse than a father who is not there for you emotionally is not having a father—whether by divorce or death. Divorce is difficult to accept. Death is final.

Similarly, it can be emotionally damaging to have a mother who is so focused on life and work that she isn't there for you. Working mothers have no choice but to leave children with a caregiver or afterschool program. I know. I had to do that with my first son.

Abandonment is real. When a mother has to drop her child off at daycare, the child perceives it as abandonment. Love must be poured into that child so he or she will not feel rejected.

I graduated from college with a bachelor of arts degree. I wrote a thesis on the development of self-esteem in children. A knowledge of psychological development is imperative in raising a child; I think it should be a required course in college to prepare future parents. At universities, we learn everything we need to start a career but nothing about how to raise a child.

ADDICTION IS BONDAGE

Another form of bondage is addiction, which is a repetitive action that can keep you from putting God first in your life. Just being too busy with life, children, homework, sports, etc., can be a form of addiction. More intense addictions include alcohol, drugs, sex, gambling, and even greed and power.

Addiction can even be something as seemingly innocent as using

Facebook and other social media to excess. I'm guilty of that one. Sometimes I will spend an hour on Facebook when I should be using the time to read, pray, or have a conversation with a friend.

Addictions are psychological in nature.

Addictions are psychological in nature. Psychology relates to the mind as well as the emotions.

How do you eliminate addictions and bondage from your life? First, get rid of all past trauma in your life, no matter how long ago it occurred. Next, have someone pray for you who believes in the power of prayer in the Name of Jesus to remove the spirit of your past trauma.

As believers in Jesus, we need to have the desire to possess the mind of Christ. We should not allow ourselves to be bound by wrong thoughts. Fortunately, you can be released from all trauma. Often, our first reaction is to dwell on the negative, but if you focus on the goodness of God, it will give you a positive outlook on life.

Jesus wore a crown of thorns so we could wear the Crown of Righteousness. Jesus can crush our mental anguish—those thoughts that destroy our peace and soundness of mind. The way to get rid of bondage and experience a total breakthrough is by learning soundness of mind.

> *For God has not given us a spirit of **fear**, but of power*
> *and of love and of a **sound mind.***
>
> —2 Timothy 1:7 (KJV)

NEGATIVE THOUGHTS KEEP YOU IN BONDAGE

Allowing negative thoughts to play in your mind over and over again will keep you in bondage. Dwelling on the wrong things can also be addicting. ANTS (automatic negative thoughts) are those continuous, never-ending thoughts that involve things like worry and hopelessness, which lead to oppression and depression.[1] If they are not stopped, that path can lead to thoughts of suicide.

You are not alone. Don't isolate yourself. That is where the enemy wants to keep you. 1 Peter 5:8 (NLT) says, "Be alert and of sober mind. Your enemy the devil prowls around like a roaring lion looking for someone to devour."

The enemy's sole purpose is to defeat you so that you are not available to fulfill your purpose for the kingdom of God. When you are consumed by worry, you are no threat to the devil and his cohorts. The enemy does not want you to walk tall on the runway with freedom and

---

1. Daniel Amen, MD, "Transform Your Thoughts—9 'Species' of ANTs," The Daniel Plan, www.danielplan.com/blogs/dp/transform-your-thoughts---9-species-of-ants/.

confidence. A breakthrough is not an option at that point unless you have the power of God to set you free. This is where you take control of your thinking. Discover how to "demolish every deceptive fantasy and insist it bow in obedience" (2 Cor. 10:5, TPT).

How can you grab a negative thought when it has no substance? I used to ask that question often.

Not long ago, I had the opportunity to test what the Corinthian verse meant. I heard devastating news that I could do nothing about: my friend was killed in an auto accident. Even though we were not close, my thoughts kept going over and over the situation.

I created scenarios of how I could fix the situation, which I couldn't. Then I continued grieving and sank into depression. Then I was reminded of that verse about demolishing negative thoughts. I talked to Jesus about it, pulled those mental concepts out of my mind, gave them to Him, and said, "I am taking those thoughts captive and making them obedient to Christ. You take care of them. I am giving them all to You. I refuse to be depressed because that's another lie of the enemy."

When those illogical thoughts would start to creep in again, I'd say, "No, I grabbed that thought. I have already given it to you, Jesus." Then I would focus on something else.

This behavior takes discipline, but you can do it. You know those feelings will creep up on you when you think about a situation again. Every time those emotions start building up, stop them. Only you have the authority. But when you are successful, your breakthrough will occur.

Just be aware of the enemy, who wants to continually derail you and push you off the runway. You must be set free from bondage so you can walk the runway of life with your head held high, with no guilt or shame hanging over you.

Being liberated from bondage to breakthrough is all about adopting a new mind-set. When you have the mind of Christ, your thoughts will change. You take on an eternal perspective. You embrace humility and let go of what has been holding you back from your destiny. You let go of pride, and stop trying to fix things on your own.

FORGIVENESS FREES US FROM BONDAGE

No matter how miserable you are right now because of various bondages of life, know that God has a perfect plan for you. He has a plan for breakthrough, boldness, and freedom.

God's anointing breaks the bondage. The word "anoint" means "to rub on, to smear." In Israel, the shepherds would anoint their sheep with oil to keep bugs off them. When you are anointed with the oil of the Holy Spirit, demons flee from you. Being anointed increases when you spend time daily in His presence. That's when bondages are broken and freedom in Christ is found.

When you are released from bondage, you will have a breakthrough.

But before that happens, you must forgive. Remember what I wrote about in the first chapter? Forgiveness is "the act of excusing a mistake or offense." Jesus said in Matthew 6:14–15, "And when you pray, make sure you forgive the faults of others so that your Father in heaven will also forgive you. But if you withhold forgiveness from others, your Father withholds forgiveness from you" (Passion translation).

If He can forgive us, we can forgive others. Forgiveness is not easy. But the Holy Spirit lives inside us. That is why we can forgive.

Forgiveness is the catalyst for a breakthrough, which can be spontaneous or come in spurts. Removing layers of pain and insecurity from your life is usually a process. If you were completely delivered from all

---

Forgiveness is the catalyst for a breakthrough.

---

grief, sorrows, and emotional pain all at once, your mind wouldn't be able to handle it. Is it possible? Yes, but that is not the norm. You must declare daily that you have been released from bondage and that the breakthrough has come.

Say out loud, "The breakthrough belongs to me."

We say this not because we are trying to hide from reality but because we walk by faith, not by what we see with our eyes. (See 2 Corinthians 5:7.) You might still be waiting for your breakthrough. But the truth is that Jesus has already claimed the victory because He is the truth. (See John 14:6.) He claimed the victory because of the cross.

The Holy Spirit is the God of the breakthrough. Experiencing a turnaround will give you comfort in knowing how much God loves you. You will walk the runway with courage and confidence.

CHAPTER 4
Illuminate Your Identity

"The eyes if your understanding being
enlightened; that you may know What is the
hope of His calling, what are the riches of
the glory of His inheritance in the saints…
which He worked in Christ when He raised
Him from the dead and seated Him at the
right hand in heavenly places…"
Ephesians 1:18–20 (NKJV)

What makes you unique? Who do you identify with? Your family? Your children? The university you graduated from? Your career? All those things contribute to your personality and what makes you who you are.

Identity is about knowing those unique characteristics and personality traits that belong only to you. You also must know who you are as a believer in Jesus Christ. You were bought with a price—Jesus died on the cross for your sins and mine. You are now reconciled and restored to God because of what Jesus did. Your position in God's kingdom is that you will be seated with Him in heaven. You will not understand where you fit in His plan unless you know in your heart that you are a child of God. When you become aware of that fact, you will be on your way to realizing your calling in the body of Christ. Ask God what your *raison d'etre*, your reason for living, is. Life is too short to guess your purpose.

Your "God identity" has to do with your awareness that you became a child of God. You were born again into His kingdom when you asked Jesus to be Lord and Savior of your life. Your new life in Christ is not about you; it is *all* about who Jesus is and how much God the Father loves you.

In his book *The Bondage Breaker,* Neil Anderson says, "It is *not* what we do that determines who we are. It is who we are that determines what we do."[1] In today's culture, many children do not have a father or mother to treat them the way God desires.

1. Neil Anderson, The Bondage Breaker (Eugene, Oregon: Harvest House Publishers, 2005).

We live in a fallen world in which life is not perfect, as God designed it to be. Children who grow up not knowing what a true father is or suffering abuse at the hands of a father find it difficult to relate to a loving, heavenly Father. It is hard to trust your divine Dad when you fear your natural father or he is not there for you.

If you had any idea how much your Abba Father loves you, you would not worry or have so much anxiety in your life about the challenges you face. Just say to Him, "Father God, I know You are in control and taking care of my life. I trust in Your love because Your Word says in 1 John 4, "God **is** love."

> *But God—so rich is He in His mercy! Because **of** and in order **to** satisfy the great and wonderful and intense **love** with which He loved us...*
> —Ephesians 2:4 (AMP)

DON'T LET INSECURITY BE YOUR IDENTITY

I grew up shy and insecure. Before my mother passed away, I learned that her father had died during a flu epidemic when she was two years old. She never bonded with her stepfather, so she did not grow up with a positive image of a father. Instead, she grew up with a sense of insecurity. And she passed it on to me.

Delete insecurity from your life. Insecurity is like wearing clothes that are drab, boring, and mismatched. The spirit of rejection and abandonment oppresses you and keeps you focused on yourself. Satan does

---

The spirit of rejection and abandonment oppresses you.

---

this to keep you from knowing your identity and destiny in God. That way, he can keep you quiet and at a standstill.

Layers of insecurity have been and continue to fall away from me as I go through life. In recent years, I have glimpsed how much God the Father loves me. Because I know I am loved, I can do what He has called me to do. I am nothing without Him, but I am everything with Him.

Now I can walk the runway of God's design dressed for success and fashioned in His likeness. It is my desire that as you continue to read this book, you will realize your value.

I used to cower when my first husband would tell me, "You are nothing but a bull in a china shop." That was his way of saying I was clumsy and unpredictable. We are no longer married. Now I know that my Father God and my current husband love me. I know I have value. I am now confident in the woman I was made to be.

Learn your identity. Know who you are in Christ. Realize that Jesus came to fulfill the law and became our new identity. We are *in* Christ as born-again believers. Discover the inheritance He has for you.

Being loved by God creates security. When you read and study the Bible, you will learn who you are in God's eyes. Jesus *is* the Word. Dwell on His promises. Write them down, memorize them, and say them out loud. He is seated at the right hand of God, constantly interceding in prayer for us.

> *It is Christ who died and furthermore is also risen,*
> *Who is even at the right hand of God, who also makes*
> *Intercession for us.*
> —Romans 8:34 (NIV)

Knowing that Jesus is praying for us daily gives us security. That promise should also free us from worry and anxiety because we know how much we are loved.

GOD CREATED US IN HIS IMAGE

Think of a model who desires to wear her favorite designer's clothes for an upcoming fashion show. She is eager for the big event. Maybe she asked the show's head coordinator of clothing if she could wear the newest Chanel designs. She can hardly wait!

Then the big day comes. She arrives at the show extra early. The truck with all the clothing drives up to the back door to drop it off. She anxiously waits for the head coordinator to arrive, and when she does, the model quickly walks over to ask about wearing the preferred clothes. The coordinator tells the model to look at the clothes being put on the rack in order of each model's turn. The model finds her name, and, yes, she has five changes…and will be wearing Chanel.

God, the ultimate Designer, wants to give you your heart's desires. He wants to give you His clothing to model on your runway of life. He wants you to shine for Him because He loves you. You represent Him on Earth. He wishes for you to walk with a spirit of excellence.

Your size does not matter. Your shape does not matter. The color of your skin does not matter. We are God's children, and all of us are beautiful in His eyes. When God sees us, He is not looking for perfection. He is looking for His reflection.

Learn to trust and obey. Remember, we can take only one step at a time. Trust in God's faithfulness. Because of the Holy Spirit, you can love other people without hesitation so they, too, can know that *extravagant* love.

> *Mostly what God does is love you. Keep company with Him and learn a life of love. Observe how Christ loved us. His love was not cautious but **extravagant**. He didn't love in order to get something FROM us but to give*

everything of Himself to us. Love like that.
—Ephesians 5:2 (MSG)

What does this have to do with your identity? Everything. Your identity is in Christ because you are fashioned in His image. Genesis 1:26 says, "Let **us** create man in **our** image."

"Our" refers to the Father, The Son, and the Holy Spirit. The trinity is composed of three persons with three personalities but are One God. This concept can be difficult for our finite minds to understand.

When you are intimate with Jesus Christ and have a personal relationship with Him through the Holy Spirit, you are His favorite. Another word for one who has favor is *grace.*

So now, brethren, I commend you to God and to the word
of His Grace, which is able to build you up and give you
an inheritance among those who are sanctified.
—Acts 20:32 (NKJV)

Sanctify means to set apart, to separate, to purify. We are God's "favorite" when we have set ourselves apart for His purpose, when we are 100 percent committed to God, no matter what.

You speak to Him all the time during the day. Ask the Holy Spirit what He thinks you should do in a situation or if He approves of what you're wearing. Is it appropriate for the occasion? When you have the Holy Spirit inside you, you will know His voice. When you speak the Word, angels are released to go and do what has been proclaimed.

The effectual fervent prayer of a righteous man avails much.

—James 5:16 (NKJV)

LET A PERSONAL RELATIONSHIP WITH JESUS DEFINE YOUR IDENTITY

God did not create us to be mannequins. He gives us a choice to follow Him or not. Just as He loves you, He wants you to love Him out of relationship, not religion.

Religion says, "Do this, or don't do that, or else." Relationship says, "Because You love me and I love you, I will honor You, Jesus, by living in obedience according to Your Word." In the Old Testament, the Israelites were commanded to "love the LORD your God with all your heart, and with all your soul and with all your strength" (Deut. 6:5). All they had was the Law of Moses and the Ten Commandments.

However, today Christians should love the Lord God out of relationship with Jesus Christ. He came to fulfill the Law. We are in the New Covenant. The Law is our foundation, but it is grace that covers us. Grace is a Person. Grace is Jesus. "For by grace are you saved…" (Eph. 2:8). As you grow in the knowledge of who Jesus is, you are continually transformed into His image. That is your identity. You are seated with Christ in heavenly places. That is your position.

TAKING A STAND BUILDS YOUR IDENTITY

Esther was in the process of discovering her identity. She could have thought she was nothing because her parents had died when she was a little girl and left her an orphan. Thank God for her cousin, Mordecai, who took it upon himself to raise her. Growing up, she was an average Jewish girl living life in Persia. One day, King Xerxes declared that all beautiful young women in the kingdom should step forward if they wished to be considered to become the new queen. All the women considered worthy were taken into the palace to go through a year of cosmetic beauty treatments before meeting the king.

Esther had favor with Hegai, who was in charge of the harem. He taught her how to walk, talk, dress, and present herself. So when she met the king, she knew what to say—and the rest is history. Esther won

Esther won the king's favor and became Queen Esther of Persia.

the king's favor and became Queen Esther of Persia.

Mordecai told Esther, "For if you remain silent at this time, Relief and deliverance for the Jews will arise from another place, but you and your father's family will

perish. And who knows but that you have come to your

royal position for such a time as this?"

—Esther 4:14 (NIV)

Queen Esther told the king that the Jewish people were going to all be killed in a few days if he didn't act. Not only that, it was the king's right-hand man, Haman, who was planning to kill the Jews.

Esther was bold during the confrontation. She had been in obedience and preparation for that amazing showdown to take place. Her identity was established. It was illuminated.

YOUR IDENTITY IN GOD IS DETERMINED BY YOUR OBEDIENCE

In 1989, I went through a divorce with my first husband because he was gay and didn't want to be married to me anymore. While this was going on, I met weekly with a female counselor from the church I attended. She took me through a biblical study examining my positional identity in Christ. I remember meditating on Psalm 139, a good chapter about the fact that God knows everything about each of us.

I will praise You, for I am fearfully and wonderfully

made; Marvelous are Your works, and that my soul knows

very well. My frame was not hidden from You when I

was made in secret, and skillfully wrought in the lowest

parts of the earth. Your eyes saw my substance, being yet
unformed. And in Your book they all were written, the
*days **fashioned** for me when as yet there were none of*
them. How precious also are Your thoughts to me, O God!
How great is the sum of them!
—Psalm 139:14–17

That Scripture made me feel important to God. Even though I was being rejected by my husband, God showed me that He accepted me, loved me, and knew every detail about me. My identity is in Christ.

Since that time, I have met a wonderful man who truly loves me, and we have been married for more than twenty-six years. I want to encourage you to never give up.

God has a wonderful plan for your life. He has already planned your destiny. It's all about obedience to King Jesus. It is up to you to listen to the Holy Spirit and prepare for it.

How do you do that? Every day, spend time with God. I like to abbreviate that to "TWG," and I type it on the calendar on my cell phone. The more you read and study the Word, the more you will understand your identity.

Each of us has a scroll or a book in heaven that describes our purpose and destiny. Worship opens your book.

The world operates on the basis of performance-based identity.[2] People's identities are focused on "who I am and what I do." If you perform well, you are accepted. If you fail, you will feel worthless. This mindset is based on perfectionism. Either you work really hard to be perfect, or you are afraid of failure and therefore avoid work. But this focus on self will never make a person happy.

When you know who you are and your identity in Christ, you will discover your purpose and calling. You will know you have value because you will know your Abba Father loves and accepts you. You will experience true joy.

You will have boldness and confidence to walk the runway God has designed for you. That design has already determined your destiny. All you need to do is trust the Holy Spirit to give you direction and light your way. Your identity is then illuminated.

---

2. "Performance-Based Self-Identity," Life Counseling Solutions, www. lifecounselingsolutions.com/2014/05/performance-based-self-identity.

CHAPTER 5
Guilt Be Gone, Shame Be Shattered

"There is therefore now no condemnation
for those who are in Christ Jesus, who
walk not according to the flesh, but
according to the Spirit."
Romans 8:1–2 (MEV)

Everyone at some point in his or her life has to deal with guilt. Guilt causes you to say, "I need to be forgiven because I did something bad." Guilt is good when the Holy Spirit convicts you of sin or an iniquity you are guilty of committing. But guilt can be damaging when you ask for God's forgiveness and then continue to beat yourself up because you sinned.

DON'T LET GUILT CONDEMN YOU

The word "sin" comes from the Greek word *hamartia,* which is an archery term meaning "missing the mark." Continuous sin is bondage. Continuous sin is an addiction.

Sin is when you mess up but immediately confess and stop. *Iniquity* is when you continually do what is wrong without stopping. But when guilt nags at you even though you have confessed your sins to Jesus, guilt can lead you into a spirit of condemnation.

Have you ever felt a tugging at your heart saying that you were guilty of something? Have you repented of your wrongdoings and asked Jesus Christ for forgiveness?

1 John 1:9 (NIV) says, "If we confess our sins, He is faithful and just to forgive us our sins and purify us from *all* unrighteousness." No more guilt! If it comes back into your thoughts, say to yourself, "Oh, no, you don't. I was forgiven and set free on [*fill in the date*]. Leave now!" When you have been forgiven, the spirit of condemnation is another lie

from Satan to keep you pressed down, shoved under, and pushed back.

DON'T LET SHAME DEFINE YOU

Shame is another lie and evil spirit. When guilt says, "I did something bad," shame says, "I *am* bad." Guilt focuses on behavior; shame

---

Shame is another lie and evil spirit.

---

focuses on self. Guilt says, "I'm sorry; I made a mistake." Shame says, "I *am* a mistake."

Shame is a combination of fear and pride. Shame is the fear of being exposed and hurt again. Shame is pride because you have built an imaginary wall to protect your self-esteem. Shame can shatter your true identity in God and rob you of your joy.

Brené Brown, PhD, a prominent licensed clinical social worker, says, "Shame is the swampland of the soul. The less you talk about your shame, the more you have it." She says that "being vulnerable is the only way to get rid of shame."[1]

Being vulnerable is a key to living a life of stability and wholeness. Being vulnerable is not a weakness, as many tend to think. Instead, it allows you to be susceptible to being wounded again. But because you have let go of shame, being vulnerable is a sign of strength.

Being open and honest about your pain will help you heal. If you don't get rid of shame, it can lead to depression, anxiety, addictions, and even suicide. Shame is an epidemic in our culture.

FIVE EXAMPLES OF PEOPLE WHO SUFFERED SHAME IN THE BIBLE

The Bible tells of many who suffered shame. Here are five.

- **Adam and Eve**—They felt shame after they ate the fruit of the tree of the knowledge of good and evil. (See Genesis 3:7.) Eve was alone in the Garden of Eden when the serpent deceived her into eating the forbidden fruit. God had identified one tree that Adam and Eve should not take fruit from, but they did it anyway. The devil put doubt in Eve's mind about God's Word. She succumbed to the temptation and gave the fruit to Adam to eat. Immediately, they both realized that they were naked, and suddenly they were full of shame because of their nakedness. God

---

1. Brené Brown, "The Power of Vulnerability," 2011 TED Talk, https://www. youtube.com/watch?v=iCvmsMzlF7o.

made coverings for them out of animal skin. This not only covered their shame in the natural world but also was symbolized the cross and the Blood of Jesus covering our sin.

- **Moses**—He felt shame after he accidently killed an Egyptian and ran away into the wilderness. Moses was an Israelite born during the time when King Herod he was killing all baby boys under the age of two. His mother put him in a quilted basket and floated him down the river. Pharaoh's daughter found him and asked if she could raise him. Pharaoh allowed her to do so. After Moses grew up, he learned of his real heritage. He then desired to help save the Israelites from slavery in Egypt. One day, he saw an Israelite being beaten by an Egyptian. Anger overtook Moses, and he accidently killed the Egyptian. Because of fear and shame, Moses ran away to an area called Midian. Later, God used Moses to deliver the Israelites. Moses's shame disappeared when God parted the Red Sea for the million people to cross over on dry land. (See Exodus 2:14 and Exodus 14.)

- **King David**—He felt shame when he had sex with Bathsheba, murdered her husband, and was responsible for the baby who died. That day, David should have been with his soldiers in battle. Instead, he relaxed at home. While on the rooftop of the palace, he saw a beautiful woman bathing. No man should have been in sight of her, but David saw this woman and lusted after her. He sent someone to call her to the palace, where they had sex. Bathsheba became pregnant. Full of shame, David had her husband killed on the battlefield. Nathan, the prophet, confronted the king and exposed what happened. The baby was born but became ill. David repented, fasted, and prayed for the baby to live. God does not always give us what we want, even though we have repented of our sins. There are consequences in the natural realm. Thank God for His mercy…but His plan is often very different than our human way of thinking. By the time the child died, David had let go of his shame. He married Bathsheba, who later gave birth to Solomon. (See 2 Samuel 11–12.)

- **Rahab, the prostitute**—She felt shame regarding her lifestyle. Two spies from Israel were sent to scout out Jericho. They met Rahab on the street and befriended her. The spies went to her house and discussed what the Israelites were going to do to the city. The three of them made an agreement that her family would be spared if she protected them from the King of Jericho. Rahab's shame was healed because she obeyed the God of Israel. (See Joshua 2.) She eventually married one of the men who saved her family.

- **Samson**—He felt shame when he was a judge for Israel and fell in love with a Philistine named Delilah. She did not love Samson, and she deceived him into telling her why he had supernatural strength. When he told her the truth, he lost all power because God left him. Samson eventually told Delilah that the true secret to his strength was is in his long hair. She cut it when he was asleep and called in the guards, who waited to kidnap him. He had allowed himself to get into a compromising position and paid the price. He was put in prison. But God used Samson to deliver the Israelites because his heart was right. Although he was full of shame, Samson showed God how much he loved Him by sacrificing his life. In Judges 16, we read about Samson's hair growing back again and how the resulting strength reinvigorated him. He was able to pull two pillars of the Philistines' temple to Dagon, causing the structure to crumble and killing all who were there. Samson's hair grew back, which allowed God to anoint him one last time.

God can use you today in positive ways, no matter what you have done in the past.

These examples of shame come from the Old Testament. Today, we have much shame in our culture. If you don't get rid of shame, it will continue to intimidate you. Shame keeps you isolated, which can lead to depression. What you do not face and deal with will always remain the same.

SHAME IS A FORM OF ADDICTION

I know of a mother who was filled with shame. I will call her Amy. Her daughter, Michelle, age fifteen, got drunk one night and got pregnant. She had been hanging around the wrong crowd and became rebellious. Four months later, her belly began to show. The evidence would be impossible to hide much longer.

Amy couldn't talk with anyone about this situation. Because she was a Christian, shame over the incident consumed her. She thought, "What? My daughter? She grew up in a Christian home, attended church every Sunday, and went to summer church camp because she wanted to. What happened? What did I do wrong? Did I not raise her right? Oh, my God, what would people think if they knew my daughter got pregnant out of wedlock?"

Amy asked the Lord for answers. As the mom healed from the shame, she realized that what her daughter had done was not Mom's fault. Michelle hung out that night with the wrong person and made a bad decision. Unfortunately, this is a common occurrence. Moms need to love their sons and daughters, no matter what. Only true love will heal the heart.

When Amy was free of shame, she was able to talk to others without being embarrassed. She realized that dealing with these issues is just a part of life. Today, even her daughter has gotten rid of her shame. Amy has a beautiful granddaughter, too.

Getting rid of shame is a miracle because shame is an addiction. When internalized, it causes you to have a shame-based identity. When this happens, it can be broken only by a stronger force. That strength can be self-discipline with the support of a person or a group to help keep you in line. God is also part of that force.

I can relate to Amy quite a bit. My oldest son was in and out of prison for twelve years. One night, he got drunk and couldn't think right. He made a wrong decision and was arrested.

When he was first going through the legal system, I went by myself to every court session he had to deal with. I visited him in jail once a week. Prison was different. It was very far away. But I prayed for him all the time and wrote letters.

I realized that my son's arrest was not about me.

As time went on, I realized that my son's arrest was not about me. It was about decisions he had made on his own. He was an adult. We all need to realize that decisions we make affect many people, not just us.

When he messed up on parole in 2016, the judge wanted to sentence him to eight years in prison. It was my son's third offense. His psychologist, whom I had been going to, made a timeline of his life to prove that my son was not a criminal. She showed his life, what happened when, and why he responded the way he did. When his attorney presented it to the judge, the judge decided to give my son less than three years. That was a miracle!

My son was released from prison earlier this year. He had been set free from alcohol and drugs. He went through the Narcotics Anonymous (NA) program. He was doing well and working two jobs. He was happy and looking forward to getting on with life. But then in September 2018, he was found collapsed. My son had died from a massive heart attack. He was only thirty-five years old. I knew he had high blood pressure. He had gained weight with all the good food that he hadn't had in prison. In the past, he had been on methamphetamine, which I found out enlarges your heart.

In thinking about what possibly happened, I have come to the conclusion that the heart is greater than the habit. My son loved Jesus and had the Holy Spirit in his heart. The spirit can overrule the soul's addiction. But often, the flesh gets tempted and can't say no. The state of the heart is more important than the activity. God knows our hearts.

A week before my son died, I asked him, "So, what do you think God's calling is on your life?"

He responded, "I want to travel the world like you do and share Jesus."

Shortly after my husband and I got the word about our son's death, I thought about what he had said. I was sad because what he wanted to do with his life was not going to happen. Four days later, it occurred to me that my son *was* doing what God was calling him to do: he is traveling the world through me! I often tell his story in my presentations. People are getting set free.

PEOPLE WEAR MASKS TO HIDE SHAME AND GUILT

Guilt and shame can weigh heavy on a person's shoulders. When people are consumed by guilt and shame, they rarely smile. Their eyes don't meet other people's eyes. They pay little attention to cleanliness. They wear invisible masks to hide the pain, putting on a happy face so others won't know they are suffering.

Fashion models often wear those invisible masks every time they are on the runway. To the runway audience, they appear to be confident, accomplished models. But often, underneath that disguise are guilt, shame, and anorexia. They often hear they are too fat, even though they are far from being overweight. Often, they are pressured to lose more weight or face the end of their modeling careers.

This is the same as in real life, only in different forms. Many people are wearing masks in their own walks of life. People are expected to look a certain way and behave a certain way. They pretend to be some-one they are not.

But when we learn to walk in love, we can be God's fashion models wherever we go.

No longer do we need to feel insecure, inadequate, and full of shame. No longer do we have to wear the mask. God accepts us, no matter what. Weight, ethnicity, and age are of no consequence. Are we perfect? No. Are we going to mess up? Yes, of course. But when we do, we just need to ask forgiveness and get back in line with His design for our lives.

When shame and guilt have been eradicated from your being, you are in a position to walk the runway of life with happiness and freedom. The weight of guilt and shame no longer hold you down. Your shoulders are relaxed. You can hold your head up high and stand straight and tall.

CHAPTER 6
No More Mannequins

"Jesus said, 'And My life is on
display in them.'"
—John 17:10 (MSG)

Boutiques and department stores often use mannequins to display clothing and accessories. The mannequins have perfect bodies. That can send subliminal messages to us that if we don't look like the mannequins, which are held up as the ideal standard, then we are lacking. That can do a number on our self-esteem.

A few days before Father's Day 2017, my husband and I were at a shopping mall. A mannequin on display was meant to look like a father with a belly. We laughed and took a picture of my husband pointing at his stomach next to the fake guy decked out for Father's Day.

Despite our having fun with the out-of-shape mannequin, we, as Christians, should be a display of His glory, a model of the Lord Jesus Christ. Many times, you will be the only example of Jesus that people know. Are you loving? Kind? Considerate?

BE A MODEL FOR THE KINGDOM OF GOD

If you are 100 percent committed to God, no matter what, you are a wondrous working warrior in the Kingdom of God. You will present yourself to those around you with a spirit of integrity regarding the way you serve your family, your business, and your community. You are to be a model for, an example of, the Kingdom of God. You are not a dummy or a mannequin.

A mannequin is a life-sized model of a man, woman, or child. In the past, they were made of plastic or *papier-mâché* materials. Today, most mannequins are made of fiberglass. A dismantled mannequin has detachable arms and legs. Mannequins can also be headless.

As human models of Jesus Christ, it is important for us not to be fake, plastic, or headless in our thinking. We need to be examples of

---

We need to be examples of God, our Designer.

God, our Designer. He created us in His image. He designed us in His likeness.

FAITH IN GOD MELTS AWAY THE ANGUISH

Fashion models are real, but many of them live in a fantasy world. They place an imaginary wall in front of them to protect their self-esteem and not let anyone see their shame or insecurities.

You don't have to be a fashion model to have an invisible wall covering up your true identity. I would guess that at least 80 percent of people put up barriers to hide who they really are. The walls they put up are intended to shield them from emotional pain and protect them from getting hurt again.

Knowing Jesus and acknowledging His love for you will gently eradicate the layers of mental anguish you might have acquired. Worrying constantly is anguishing. Thinking you are the only one who can fix a situation weighs heavy on your psyche. But as your trust in God increases, the layers of distress will start to disappear. God is kind enough to emotionally heal you, little by little. Your load of heaviness will get lighter and lighter. Worshipping and spending time reading the Bible will heal your soul. Built-up walls of fear and pride will crumble. I encourage you to memorize a few Scriptures so that you can speak them out loud in the car or wherever. Here is an extremely comforting verse:

When you pass through the waters, I will be with you:
And through the rivers, they shall not overflow you. When
you walk through the fire you shall not be burned, Nor
shall the flame scorch you.
—Isaiah 43:2 (NKJV)

Aren't those soothing words? I remember reading that verse aloud when I went through a hard time in regard to our business. The IRS audited our company, combing through three years of charitable donations. I remember getting the letter. Before I opened it, I held it up high and said, "Jesus, you know our business belongs to you. Whatever this letter is asking, I give it to You to take care of. I will not stress about it."

I never had any fearful thoughts. I knew my God would oversee the situation. I answered all the questions and provided all the copies needed to show the IRS we were in compliance. We came out with the best rating you can have in an audit. Thank God for His Word and His exceedingly great and precious promises.

SURROUND YOURSELF WITH PEOPLE WHO LOVE YOU

When you are down, depressed, and discouraged, I encourage you not to be alone. We were not created to be isolated. That's exactly how the devil wants you—alone. He wants us all to be alone and disconnected from other people. Get involved in a local Bible-believing church where you can hear the Word and meet other people of like faith.

Years ago, our pastor delivered a message about Judges 18. A tribe of Israel spied on their enemies to see if it was safe to go and conquer them. The spies discovered that the Sidonians lacked a ruler. Verse 7 says, "They had no ties with anyone." Verse 27 tells us that because they had no leader, "They struck them with the edge of the sword and burned the city with fire." There was no deliverer for the city of Sidon because they had "no ties with anyone." They were not connected with another community.

Friendships and connections with people are important. Unfortunately, people isolate themselves for many reasons. For one thing, life is really busy. Maybe they are so stressed from work and life's challenges that they are too tired, mentally and physically, to socialize. They need to be with other believers, but maybe they are too insecure to go alone. Maybe health reasons keep them away.

To immerse yourself in God's love, mercy, and grace, find a church where you feel comfortable, a church full of people whose company you enjoy. The point is to go to a church where you are celebrated, not just tolerated.

People who love you are essential to your well-being. You need them to speak truth into your life. They can't do that if you are disconnected from them.

Being alone is unwise and unsafe. Isolation will make you vulnerable to the enemy. When you are by yourself, your mind goes over and over painful events and how they could have or should have been different. Those thoughts, if you do not stop them, will create negative pathways of neurons in your brain.

Loneliness comes from shame. Shame comes from fear. Fear says that other people will not accept you if they really knew who you are and what you have done. When you don't feel loved, depression sets in.

Love is the answer. God is love. Only love will heal depression.

> *There is no fear in love, but perfect love casts out fear,*
> *because fear has to do with punishment. Whoever fears is*
> *not perfect [mature] in love.*
> —1 John 4:18 (MEV)

THE MIND IS THE BATTLEFIELD

Satan will put wrong thoughts in your mind. It is up to you to discern these thoughts through the Word of God. If you have trouble with that, renew your mind as Romans 12:2 instructs us to do. Make a decision to transform wrong thinking so it aligns with God's design.

In her book *Battlefield of the Mind*, Joyce Meyer, president of Joyce Meyer Ministries, states that we are in a war, and that "our warfare is not with other human beings but with the devil and his demons." She writes, "Our enemy, Satan, attempts to defeat us with strategy and de-

Satan attempts to defeat us with strategy and deceit.

ceit, through well-laid plans and deliberate deception."[1]

I know from personal experience that this is true. Years ago, I was being tempted by thoughts that would compromise my belief system. I knew what I was thinking about was wrong, but I kept trying to justify my thoughts. The enemy has much experience trying to bring us down. This particular time, he tried hard to push me off the runway of God's

1. Dr. Joyce Meyer, *Battlefield of the Mind: Winning the Battle in Your Mind* (New York: Warner Books, 1995), 11.

design. But I did not give in. I saw that the devil was trying to destroy my life. He was trying to make me feel sorry for myself. He was attempting to entice me with a worldly lifestyle instead of what I have been called to do. Living for Jesus is not always easy. But the rewards of doing so far surpass this world we live in. Focus forward. Make your thoughts align with God's design. Don't let the enemy destroy your destiny.

It takes self-control, which, by the way, is a fruit of the Holy Spirit. Don't let your emotions control you. Let your born-again spirit be in charge, and tell your emotions how they will behave. God has given you clarity of mind. That's a promise.

> *For God has not given us a spirit of fear, But of power*
> *and of love and of a sound mind.*
> —2 Timothy 1:7 (NKJV)

The more you worship and spend time in His presence, the greater relationship you will have with the Holy Spirit. The more you speak the Word, the more you will realize how valuable you are to God. Realizing how precious you are in Christ will give you boldness and confidence. He knew you before the foundations of the world. (See Ephesians 1:4.) He has an amazing plan for you and your destiny. Read Luke 12:22–25 to start learning of your eternal value. In fact, I encourage you to memorize that passage of Scripture.

Why are you worth so much to God? The reason is that you were created in His image. You were fashioned in His likeness, not as a mannequin, a dummy, or a robot.

[The Lord Jesus Christ]: Who will transform our humble bodies and transfigure us into the identical likeness of His glorified body.

—Philippians 3:21 (TPT)

Only the Lord Jesus has the power to change us to be fashioned in the likeness of His glorious body. We must reflect who He is in us wherever we go.

God has a purpose for your life. God will use your unique qualities to be a model for Him. Yes, you are unique. Your spirit, soul, and body are not like anyone else's. No one has your mind, your personality, or your looks. When you accept your God identity, you will be a confident, genuine model of His Kingdom.

CHAPTER 7
Dress for Success

"Now you're dressed in a new wardrobe.
Every item of your new life is custom-made
by the Creator, with His label on it. All the
old fashions are now obsolete."
Colossians 3:10 (MSG)

The way you dress sends a message to others. You make an impression on the people who look at you. Dressing well shows respect and honor. As believers, we are ambassadors for the kingdom of God (KOG). We are His KOG agents, His wonder-working warriors, His representatives.

Decide you want to be successful. Be motivated to be the best at whatever you do in life. Motivational speaker Jim Rohn said, "Motivation is what gets you started. Habit is what keeps you going."

When you are motivated, make a decision to do what you need to do to make it happen. Then take action, and make action a habit.

SET GOALS TO GAIN MOTIVATION

You will become motivated when you plan toward your goals. Think of what you would like to accomplish in the next five years, one year, six months, one week, and today. Being organized and objective-oriented is the inward part of dressing for success. You don't want to just look good on the outside but have no inward incentive for greatness. Write down more than just a list; include how you plan to achieve each goal. Write down the actions you will need to take. Then do something every day to see those concepts become reality. When you do this, you form a habit. Good habits create opportunities.

When my husband was in college, he started to daydream about how he could make money. He wasn't interested in English or physics.

He focused only on going out and making it happen. That's the entrepreneur in him. He began by taking office-maintenance jobs at nights. When he got too busy, he hired helpers. He'd come home in the wee hours of the morning, grab a little food from the refrigerator, and flip on the TV. Infomercials showed viewers how to make it rich in real estate with no money down. He didn't know how that could happen.

After a few weeks of watching those infomercials, he took a job at a title company to learn how to search properties and read the titles. A few years later, he felt confident enough to start his own company. He made a habit of getting up every morning, seeing what was going up for sale, reading the titles, and going to look at the properties. If he liked a property, he'd attend the trustee sale and place a bid. He did that time and time again.

His goal of making money motivated him. His plan to make it happen became a habit. That was thirty-three years ago. He ended up becoming an extremely successful in his business pursuit.

Do what you are good at. Motivate yourself and form habits to accomplish your goals.

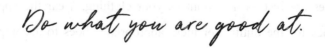

Do what you are good at.

DRESSING WELL HELPS ESTABLISH YOUR IMAGE

Dressing for success creates an image. In business, if you want to influence people in the office, you dress a certain way. For a man, this could be dress shirt with a blazer and khaki pants. A suit and tie always look good. My father was a doctor. He wore a suit and tie six days a week.

For a woman, business dress can be a sheath dress with a blazer. A knee-length pencil-cut skirt with a buttoned-down blouse and blazer is another good choice. Nice pants with heels are also acceptable.

If you look good, you will feel good.

If you look good, you will feel good. You will feel like performing well.

Shoes are just as important as your clothing. Wear the appropriate shoes for the outfit. For men, appropriate shoes to accompany a business-casual ensemble can include leather loafers or leather Oxford shoes. For women in business, casual dress shoes, pumps, stilettos, or closed-toe kitten heels are acceptable. Ballet flats or strappy sandals are not appropriate as business wear.

What shoes have you been wearing? The shoes of a soccer mom? The shoes of a student? The shoes of an entrepreneur? The shoes of a business executive?

Step into someone else's shoes, and see life from their viewpoint. What have they been walking through?

PUT ON THE ARMOR OF GOD

You put on a new wardrobe when you accepted Jesus Christ as your Savior. You put on the garments of salvation and the robes of righteousness. (See Isaiah 61:10.) You slipped on the shoes of the Gospel of Peace. You were clothed in His righteousness. You declared righteousness when the Holy Spirit came to dwell inside your spirit. Righteousness is a person. Righteousness is Jesus. You are righteous because the righteous One lives inside you.

Being dressed for success is ultimately being clothed with the salvation of the Lord Jesus Christ.

> *Rather, clothe yourselves with the Lord Jesus Christ, and do not think about how to gratify the desires of the flesh.*
> —Romans 13:14 (NIV)

Dressing for success means being covered by His glory. It is putting on the presence of God in worship. It is speaking the Word and putting on the full armor of God every morning before you leave your home. (See Appendix A.)

When you have vocally put on the full armor of God, you are completely dressed for success—in the supernatural world. You will be profitable in prayer because you are wearing the weapons of righteousness. Remember that confession is possession. You can have what you say.

When you are successful in His kingdom, He will make you effective in your sphere of influence.

CLOAK YOURSELF IN THE HOPE OF ETERNAL LIFE

I once talked with our attorney about eternity and accepting Jesus. I told him that when you die, that's it. There is no appeal. Being an attorney, he totally understood what the word meant. He said, "Hmm…I'll think about it." I truly hope he decided to follow Jesus before he passed away in 2009. If I hadn't been a successful businesswoman, that opportunity to talk with him about Jesus would have never come to pass.

The Word says, "NOW is the day of salvation" (2 Cor. 6:2). If you keep putting it off, you will be distracted by life. Then it could be too late.

Hope for an eternal life is required if you want to be bold and strong in the Lord. That is why you need the power of the Holy Spirit in your life. I became a Christian when I asked Jesus into my heart at age six. I rededicated my life to Him when I was thirteen. Since then, I have never turned away from God. He has proven Himself faithful to me more times than I could count.

When my first husband abandoned my son and me, I could have easily been paralyzed by fear, anxiety, and stress. But even during that hard time in my life, I continued to trust in Jesus and His Word. I knew He would guide me in handling the details of the divorce. My main concern was to provide protection and continuity for my son. That was paramount. Everything worked out within a year without my breaking down emotionally. God showed me His faithfulness. I was successfully dressed in His goodness.

BAPTISM OF THE HOLY SPIRIT: SPEAKING IN TONGUES

I had the Holy Spirit *in* me, but I was never taught about the baptism of the Holy Spirit coming *on* me.

> *But you shall receive power when the Holy Spirit comes*
> *ON you.*
> —Acts 1:8 (NIV)

This baptism is an event. It is a time when you ask God for the power and authority of the Holy Spirit to come on you. You ask for a refreshing of His presence and your prayer language. That language is not English or your native language. Instead, that language is supernatural. It is your vocal chords, your lips forming the words, but the special language comes from the Holy Spirit inside you.

You speak mysteries that only the Almighty God and His angels understand. The demonic realm has no clue what you are saying. That is one reason why it is imperative to pray in tongues daily. Learning to pray in your prayer language is similar to a baby learning how to talk. At first, the words sound like gibberish. But the more you pray in tongues, the more mature your prayer tongue becomes.

> *How much more will your heavenly Father give the Holy Spirit to those who **ask** Him?*
> —Luke 11:13 (NIV)

The beginning of Luke 11 is where Jesus taught His disciples how to pray the Lord's Prayer.

On Sunday morning, October 3, 1993, I asked Father God to baptize me with the Holy Spirit coming *upon* me, as described in Acts 1:8. I asked for my prayer language.

You receive boldness when the Holy Spirit comes on you. My natural personality is more reserved. But when the anointing on my calling is strong, I become bolder. So, too, will you when you represent Him, His kingdom, and His fashion. You must be properly clothed for any occasion. "Be ready in season and out of season…" (2 Tim 4:2).

In 2017, I met someone on an airplane who had been fighting cancer for three and a half years. The cancer had metastasized into five of his organs. I needed the words to let him know he did not have to face this trauma alone. I told him to believe in the God of miracles, and I told him that Jesus is the healer. I asked if I could pray for him. When he said I could, I prayed for Jesus to show him how much he is loved. I prayed the story of salvation. I cursed the cancer and spoke healing and resurrection of life to every cell of his body. The man was encouraged to have a stranger tell him of God's love and pray for his healing. You have the power and ability to do the same thing.

SHARE JESUS'S LOVE WITH OTHERS

When you share the love of Jesus, you have been "clothed with strength and dignity" (Prov. 31:25). The Hebrew word for "clothing" is *labash*. The dictionary definition is to "properly wrap around, that is (by implication) to put on a garment or clothe literally or figuratively—in apparel, clothed with, come upon, put (on, upon), wear."

A well-known preacher once said, "The clothing truly makes the man or woman. The Hebrew word for 'clothe' doesn't just mean 'garment,' but it means the Spirit of God took possession."

Put on tender mercies, kindness, humility, meekness and long-suffering, and you are dressed for success in Christ. When you put on love, you are under the ownership of Jesus Christ and the possession of the Holy Spirit. You are fashioned in His image.

> *(You) have put on the new man who is renewed in knowledge according to the image of Him who created him…*
>
> —Colossians 3:10 (NKJV)

THE DETERIORATION OF FASHION AND MORALS

The fashion industry is interesting to observe. The seasons of fashion have come and gone in cycles for years. In the 1950s, women wore A-line dresses with a small belt around the waist. The men wore gray or black suits with white shirts and skinny ties. And don't forget the *chapeau*, a stylish hat. In the 1960s, men wore button-down cardigan sweaters with suit pants and dress shoes. They still wore suits, but the ties were a bit wider and often striped. The women in the 1960s wore elegant dresses after the image of Jackie O. The younger women were thrilled with the ultra-miniskirts and knee-high boots made popular by the supermodel Twiggy.

We will forever remember the huge bell-bottom pants and psychedelic prints of the 1970s. Men wore polyester suits. The ties were wider with an even thicker stripe.

Jeans for men have been popular since the 1950s. For women, from the 1960s and beyond, jeans of various styles have been worn. The 1970s is when the term "pantsuits" for both men and women came into vogue. Both men and women favored patterned dress shirts.

Color-coordinated sweat suits for men and women became the rage in the 1980s. Men's suits became more conservative again, with the ties becoming narrower. In the 1990s jeans for women were waist-high and a bit baggy. Some women showed their stomach or back skin.

The 2000s brought back miniskirts and bell-bottom jeans, now called "flares." Skinny jeans became popular toward the end of the 2000s. To-

---

Today, fashion is whatever you want to wear.

---

day, fashion is whatever you want to wear. If it's a 1950s dress, go for it. The 1960s business dress for women is also popular today. So are conservative suits for men and metro suits with high-water pant lengths and skinnier pant legs. Skinny jeans and flare jeans are both acceptable. Jeans with big holes and rips in the thighs and knees are popular. You can pay $150 for the most ripped, "distressed" jeans out there.

I believe that the decline in morality coincides with fashion that has been getting uglier. In the 1980s, baggy clothes and oversized flannel shirts were popular with young people. I recently read that oversized clothes are coming back into fashion. This time, the clothes will be made of nicer material. Designers will compete for the look "large and in charge." It's as if the more rebellious people are, the sloppier their clothes have become.

Wear it all, or focus on one decade if you wish. I have seen women stick to the 1950s, not only in what they wear but in how they decorate their homes.

Because you now represent Jesus Christ on this planet, you must be dressed for success everywhere you go. This applies to the natural world and the supernatural world. Be appropriate for every occasion. Be full of God's Word so you will have the right words at the right time for the right person. Talk with proper speech, and walk with your head held high in boldness and confidence as God's KOG agent.

> *(He) has made us kings and priests to His God and*
> *Father, to Him be glory and dominion forever and ever.*
> *Amen.*
> —Revelation 1:6 (MEV)

Jesus Christ made us to be kings and priests, even while we are here on Earth. Kings represent those in business whose purpose it is to give money to the Kingdom of God. Gifts are seeds of righteousness being planted wherever we go.

Kings also represent Christians in positions of authority in education, government, media, and other areas. Priests are those who are apostles, prophets, evangelists, pastors, and teachers. (See Ephesians 4:11.)

> *But you are a chosen race, a royal priesthood, a holy*
> *nation, a people for God's own possession, so that you*
> *may declare the goodness of Him who has called you out*
> *of darkness into His marvelous light.*
> —1 Peter 2:9 (MEV)

We have been chosen to be royal ambassadors representing Jesus Christ and the Kingdom of God. That is why we should always be dressed for success.

CHAPTER 8
The Fragrance of Worship

"Pleasing is the fragrance of your perfumes;
your name is like perfume poured out."
Song of Solomon 1:3 (NIV)

When I go shopping, I often stop by the perfume counter to smell all the luscious scents. Generally, I wear a different scent every day. I like to alternate them according to my mood.

In the natural world, when you take a bath or shower, you wash yourself to get clean and fresh. You use pleasant-smelling oils, lotions, and perfumes. In the supernatural world, you are to exude the fragrances of Christ as the result of being cleansed in His presence.

> *Now thanks be to God, who always causes us to triumph*
> *in Christ, and through us reveals the fragrance of His*
> *knowledge in every place.*
> —2 Corinthians 2:14-15 (MEV)

In the Message translation (MSG), this passage reads, "Everywhere we go, people breathe in the exquisite fragrance." We are to exude the luscious-smelling perfumes of life. Daily, Jesus would go off to a quiet place and pray alone. We need to set aside time in our daily planners and do the same.

THE FOUR FRAGRANCES

In Exodus 30:23–24, we read about four fragrances. Each is important for what it represents. Here are the four fragrances that passage discusses.

Myrrh—This costly fragrance represents love. Song of Solomon 1:13 says that "a bundle of myrrh is my well beloved." Growing up, I always thought that book was about a specific romance between Solomon and his lover. Since then, I have learned that the book is a parable of how Jesus loves His Bride, His Church.

In the New Testament, John 19:39 tells how Nicodemus brought myrrh, as well as aloes, to cover Jesus's body before He was buried. They wrapped His body in linens soaked in myrrh—love.

Love for us cost Jesus His life. He could have called several angels to come and get Him off the cross. But because He trusted His heavenly

---

Love for us cost Jesus His life.

Father, He stayed there and endured the suffering. We know He rose again on the third day. Resurrection is the only reason we have hope of eternal life.

God did that because He loves us. If you had any idea how much Jesus loves you, you would not worry and fret over everyday things.

Cinnamon—This fragrance has an aroma described as "sweet." The Hebrew word for "sweet" is bosem, meaning a fragrance that is sweet and spicy. That seems like an oxymoron, but when cinnamon is added to holy anointing oil, it brings zeal and passion. Zeal in Hebrew means "jealousy."

For you shall not worship any other god, for the LORD, whose name is Jealous, is a jealous God.

—Exodus 34:14 (MEV)

Today, the Holy Spirit wants you to spend time with Him. Jesus is jealous for your time. In my study, I have a stuffed chair. I often think of Jesus sitting there, waiting patiently for me. But I am running around putting out "fires," doing everything else, when I need to acknowledge that Jesus is One who can extinguish all fires.

When it is your heart's desire to be cleansed and purified, zeal will become a part of your being. Zeal is the idea of "being eagerly in pursuit of" something. It is the very picture of being filled with intense desire.

Zeal for Your house consumes me.
—John 2:17 (TMG)

The Holy Spirit dwells in your being, which is God's temple. Your house is God's house.

Calamus—This fragrance, thought to mean "reed," is from a plant that grows along the banks of rivers. This plant has a crown and is full of spines or thorns. Calamus will emit its fragrance only when crushed. In Arabic, this word means "to cut or to pare." Calamus is symbolic of weakness. Leviticus 2:16 mentions that the priest burns as a memorial a part of the "memorial portion of the crushed grain and the oil…"

This is a symbol of Jesus, the Bread of Life, dying on the cross for us, being the perfect sacrifice, that bridge between sinful man and Holy God, so we can have eternal life with Him in Heaven. Jesus was bruised and crushed for our sins so we would not have to pay the penalty.

Cassia—This fragrance is the spice of devotion and consecration. The word "cassia" suggests the idea of bowing down to worship in adoration and devotion to God. "Worship" means "to honor with extravagant love and extreme submission."

Mix all the fragrances with olive oil and you have anointing oil, which is a symbol of the Holy Spirit.

WORSHIPPING HIM CREATES THE FRAGRANCE OF THE ANOINTING

When you blend love with passion and zeal, your spirit catches fire. Add to the fire adoration and humility, and you worship in a way that truly glorifies Him. It's the oil of the Holy Spirit that keeps these ingredients together. That's called "the anointing."

When you are in His presence worshipping Jesus, dying to yourself, the Holy Spirit is there, and He produces these fragrances in you. Today, these sweet-smelling perfumes come from the fruit of the Spirit that exudes from your life. There are nine fruits: love, joy, peace, patience, kindness, goodness, faithfulness, gentleness, and self-control.

These God fruits grow daily when you are supernaturally connected with Jesus Christ. During bonding times with the Holy Spirit, when His thoughts become your thoughts, the Bible will come alive to you as you read it, study it, and speak it. These actions create the fragrance of the anointing. Every ingredient in the holy anointing oil is put under extreme compression to create the most beautiful aroma possible.

As you love and adore Jesus, let Him fill you with the fragrances of the anointing oil. Your innermost being will be renewed.

You are revived and made to smell fresh in the natural world when you soak in the bathtub, quiet and relaxed. In the supernatural world, soaking is another way of saying you will wait on the Lord. Worship Him. Be absorbed in His presence.

Matthew 6 (MSG) says that when you soak, you "become like a rose, blooming and giving a fresh fragrance of God's glory wherever you go." According to the Old Testament, fragrances and pleasant aromas that pleased God the Father were burnt offerings. In Leviticus 1:9, we read about "an offering made by fire, a sweet aroma to the LORD." Why would a sacrificial lamb be a good scent to God? Burnt offerings were made in anticipation of when Jesus Christ would be born as the Son of Man on Earth. He was the Lamb of God. (See John 1:29.)

Jesus was in ministry for three years to show us how to minister. For three years, Jesus showed us how to love, teach, and heal people. Jesus exuded the fragrances of the Holy Spirit and showed us how to do the same.

The sweet fragrances of the fruit of the Holy Spirit are what exude from us when we are 100 percent committed to Jesus. The holy anointing oil of the Old Testament includes myrrh, cinnamon, calamus, and cassia, and we emit them when we have created an atmosphere of love.

Since 2005, my knowledge of God the Father, God the Son, and God the Holy Spirit has grown immensely.

My ability and desire to worship has increased. That starts with my time with God. I like to stand up, lift my hands, and close my eyes. By closing your eyes, you block out distractions. When I worship, I pray in tongues, sing songs, and pray. Often, I feel a slight heaviness come on me, making it more difficult to stand. But I try to stand anyway. Sometimes when I am in a corporate setting, I will feel tingling or buzzing in my arms. I have felt that buzzing go around my lips. When this happens, I know the anointing is powerful on me. When prophecy joins with a strong anointing, I will often collapse under the power. The presence of God is so strong, it can be virtually impossible to stand up.

When you spend time daily with God in prayer, reading the Word and worshipping, you will get into His presence much more quickly. But at first, it can take time to get rid of your focus on your flesh so you can focus on the Holy Spirit.

Learn to listen to Him. Start by asking the Holy Spirit little things, such as, "Which route home from work do you want me to take today?" "Show me who I should talk to who needs an encouraging Word." "Which outfit do You want me to wear to that event?"

Start small, and listen to Him. Over time, hearing Him will get easier.

Living the life I just described exudes the fragrance of worship. Then when you walk the runway God has prepared for you, these wonderful fragrances will ooze from your innermost being.

CHAPTER 9
Healing the Heart

"Be kind and compassionate to one another,
forgiving each other, just as in Christ God
forgave you."
Ephesians 4:32 (NIV)

To walk the runway of God's design with boldness and confidence, your heart must be healed. And healing the emotions takes time.

FORGIVENESS HEALS THE HEART

Forgiving can be a hard thing to do. When you have been hurt and violated, it can be difficult to forgive the person who mistreated you. But we must forgive because Jesus forgave us. If you don't do it, the lack of forgiveness will gnaw at your spirit.

Not forgiving can ruin your health. Bitterness is a side effect of not forgiving. Doctors call it PTED—post-traumatic embitterment disorder. One team of researchers found that the leading symptoms of PTED are "a complex negative emotional state of embitterment, anger, sadness, thoughts of revenge, helplessness, intrusive memories, and restlessness."[1]

Bitterness affects the body in several ways. Trauma can cause a hormonal imbalance; digestive disorders; and chronic pain in the head, neck, and back. The pain is caused by decreased blood flow to the cells, keeping them from absorbing nutrients. In extreme cases, the musculoskeletal system is compromised.

A lack of forgiveness is the root of much sickness, disease, and

---

1. "Diagnostic Criteria for Posttraumatic Embitterment Disorder (PTED)," Journal of Psychosomatic Research 61, no. 3 (September 2006), 402–03, https://www.researchgate.net/publication/296430052_Diagnostic_criteria_for_posttraumatic_embitterment_disorder_PTED.

bondage and causes fear, anxiety, and stress. There is a spiritual root to a prolonged failure to forgive. There is a reason you are not healed.

> *[Jesus said,] "If you forgive those who sin against you, your heavenly Father will forgive you. But if you refuse to forgive others, your Father will not forgive your sins."*
> —Matthew 6:14-15 (NLT)

THE SEVEN SPIRITS OF BITTERNESS

Dr. Henry W. Wright, in *A More Excellent Way to Be in Health,* describes seven spirits associated with bitterness: not forgiving, resentment, retaliation, anger, hatred, violence, and murder.[2]

- **Refusing to forgive someone.** You might do this continually because your spirit has been violated in your mind, your heart, or your body. In the natural world, you don't want to forgive. You might say something like, "If you knew what they did to me, you would know why I cannot forgive them." You *can* forgive. You can let go of the past.

- **Resentment.** This happens when your mind and thoughts go over and over a situation. You keep ringing the bell, so to speak, and the wounds stay fresh and raw. Dr. Wright says, "Resentment is a spiritual problem, not a psychological problem."

---

2. Henry W. Wright, *A More Excellent Way—Be in Health: Spiritual Roots of Disease, Pathways to Wholeness* (New Kensington Way, Pennsylvania: Whitaker House, 2009).

- **Retaliation.** This is the next spirit to take over. You just want to get even and show him or her a thing or two.

- **Anger.** This is the next spirit to surface in the wake of retaliation.

- **Hatred.** If anger festers long enough, the spirit of hatred shows up.

- **Violence.** This is the next rung on the downward spiral of bitter spirits.

- **Murder.** If violence isn't stopped, it can lead to this ultimate expression of bitter spirits. Murder can be either literal, or it can be "murder" with the tongue—character assassination or verbal abuse.

Not long ago, I read about a husband and wife who had recently divorced. They had two young children and shared joint custody. One day, the mom was driving the kids over to their dad's home. But she never returned home to the apartment she shared with her boyfriend of fewer than six months. The mom thought she and her ex-husband were on good terms for the children's sake. She thought wrong. About ten days later, her body was found in a plastic bag. This is an extreme example of refusing to forgive, which turned into resentment, then retaliation, then anger, then the spirit of violence, and ultimately, murder. That is called reality. That is so sad, and situations like that do not need to happen.

CORRIE TEN BOOM: A MODEL OF FORGIVENESS FOR US ALL

A woman who was able to forgive despite extreme pain was Corrie ten Boom. She was a loving Christian woman who lived in Holland. Her father, Casper ten Boom, owned a shop full of clocks and watches. The family lived above the shop in an apartment. The ten Booms were not Jewish, but they loved the Jewish people. Mr. ten Boom had a Jewish star in his storefront window as a sign that Jews were welcome at their place of business. Just before World War II started, Hitler was persecuting the Jews in their town; this was the start of the Holocaust. The Gestapo went around the village and gathered all the Jews to send them to concentration camps.

Corrie ten Boom and her family hid Jewish people in their home for quite some time, until someone betrayed them. Gestapos came in and

Gestapos came in and arrested the ten Boom family.

arrested the ten Boom family. At the time, there were two Jewish men, two Jewish women, and two resistance fighters hiding in a specially made closet. They were not caught. They stayed hidden an additional forty-seven hours until they were rescued and taken to another place. Betsy, Corrie's sister, went with her to the camps. Their father, Casper, was eighty-four years old when he was arrested. He died ten days later. For the next ten months, Corrie and Betsy were moved to three different concentration camps. Betsy, at fifty-nine, became ill and died soon after.[3]

In 1947, three years after she was eventually freed, Corrie spoke at a meeting at a church in Munich. She said, "When we confess our sins, God casts them into the deepest ocean, gone forever." A former guard who was one of the cruelest at the last concentration camp where she was held came up to her. She immediately recognized him.

"I know you know who I am, but I have become a Christian," he said. "I am cleansed from all the evil I have done. But I need you to forgive me."

He extended his hand to shake hers. Imagine for a moment the intensity that hung in the air between them. Then she held out her hand and shook his.[4]

Only God's love in your heart can lead you to forgive. If Corrie could give up her resentment, you can forgive those who have been

---

3. As described in many books, including Corrie ten Boom, *The Hiding Place* (Grand Rapids, Michigan: Chosen Books, 1971 and 1984).

4. "Break the Frozen Heart (Summer Rerun Series)," Edinburgh United Methodist Church, July 3, 2017, http://www.edinburghumc.org/blog/2017/7/3/break-the-frozen-heart-summer-rerun-series.

cruel to you as well. If you are a believer, you have Christ in your heart. He can help you to forgive.

"Forgiveness is an act of the will," Corrie ten Boom said. "The will can function regardless of the temperature of the heart."

You make a decision to forgive, even though at first your heart is cold. Speak blessings over the one who hurt you. As you allow God to heal you, your heart will warm up with love toward the person who has hurt you.

In 1975, I was traveling in the Netherlands and visited Corrie ten Boom's house. I saw the actual closet that was used to hide the Jewish people.

MY OWN JOURNEY TO FORGIVENESS

I have experienced forgiveness after being disillusioned and abandoned. Family is often our biggest disappointment. My first husband was the first major betrayal. As I mentioned, he abandoned me emotionally and physically. My brothers and their wives have seemingly rejected me. It seems that I am no longer accepted in their families. Until this year, I hadn't seen my niece and nephew in more than a decade. Their children have no idea they have an aunt and uncle who love them because they never see us.

After my parents passed away, life was different. My mother died first. My father wanted to stay in his home with everything just as it was when Mom lived there. I did everything I could to help give my dad what he needed. But my brothers talked about selling his home. As I understood it, they wanted to move my father to a nursing home because he needed 24/7 medical care. I knew that if that happened, my father would lose his will to live.

Issues arose with a bank loan to get home care, and attorneys got involved. When the dust settled, my dad got to live in his home for three more years and passed away in his bedroom, just like he wanted. Miscommunication with my brothers was a big part of our turmoil. It was a stressful time for all of us.

I learned that texting is not the way to communicate on heavy issues. My family never learned how to confront one another, let alone

---

Texting is not the way to communicate on heavy issues.

---

confront in love. We were insecure and could not come face-to-face to talk things out. We were all deeply wounded by the whole ordeal. I personally couldn't cry even if I wanted to. The tears would not come.

A few years later, I broke down my wall of pride and let my heart be healed. I forgave my brothers and their wives. I also had to forgive myself, which is the most difficult type of forgiveness. Then I was able to cry. Reconciliation still needs to take place. It has been more than a decade. It is time.

FIVE STEPS TO FORGIVENESS

In *The Freedom Factor*, Dr. Bruce Wilkinson mentions that not forgiving is a "matter of discipline, not punishment."[5] The continuous pain you go through is a result of the failure to forgive. Dr. Wilkinson offers five steps to help you on your journey to forgive.

- **Open your heart to forgive.** If you forgive from your head only, it will not last. Your emotions or your heart were hurt. If you allow your thoughts to go over and over the event, continuous meditation will become a negative pattern that will eventually spiral out of control.

- **Extend compassion to the person who wounded you.** Dr. Wilkinson says that "compassion is the door to forgiveness." Kindness and love in your heart come only from God, who created you to be fashioned in His image. Remember that you are forgiving the person, not the evil he or she did to you. That is key. Jesus forgave *us* of our sins at the cross, not the sins themselves.

---

5. Bruce Wilkinson, *The Freedom Factor* (Portland, Oregon: Zeal Books, 2016).

- **Release the person from your "heart prison."** Not being able to forgive keeps you in emotional slavery. I encourage you to think of who you need to forgive so you can break down that wall that is keeping you from freedom. Visualize separating the person from the offenses committed.

- **Forgive the person for each wrongdoing, offense, mistake, and wound.** Be specific. List each offense with each person on your list. I know, that might take a while. But it will be worth it. "Incomplete forgiveness is still unforgiveness, and the legal contract will not be annulled," Dr. Wilkinson says. "You must release the person separately from forgiving the wounds. The first half is *who* you release, and the second half is *what* you forgive."

- **Bless and do good to the person.** Forgiveness can come only from the Throne of Grace. The Holy Spirit who lives inside of you will help you.

I encourage you to make a list of people who have harmed you. Release their offenses verbally to God. Say out loud that you have forgiven them. Bitterness and resentment will fall off you like rocks in a landslide. You will stand tall, and the weight of the world will be taken off you. You no longer need to wear the world on your shoulders. Give each situation to Jesus by saying, "I belong to You, Jesus; take this pain from me as I forgive. Heal my heart as I obey Your Word." It is a matter of faith to forgive. Declare it. When those thoughts and feelings come back, mentally grasp them and say, "I have forgiven [*name the person*]. I walk in forgiveness. Those thoughts and feelings are lies and must leave now, in the name of Jesus."

> *Forgive us the wrongs we have done as we ourselves*
> *release forgiveness to those who have wronged us.*
> —Matthew 6:12 (TPT)

When you have forgiven those on your list, ask God to forgive you of any sins, offenses, or wrongdoing that you are guilty of committing. You must pardon others before you exonerate yourself. Forgiveness of others and yourself is a process that does not need to take much time but often does. When you forgive, your heart is in position to receive God's love. Earlier I mentioned a legal contract having power if you are unable to completely pardon someone. This legal contract has to do with the devil being the accuser. (See Revelation 12:10.)

I learned during the summer of 2017 about the Courts of Heaven and what goes on there. As Christians, we must learn to enter the gates of Heaven with thanksgiving and praise. (See Psalm 100.) The Courts of Heaven are like the courts we have here on Earth. You have the defendant (yourself), prosecutor (Satan), and mediator (Jesus Christ). Also present are an advocate or attorney (Holy Spirit), a court reporter (angels who write in your scroll or book in Heaven), and God, the judge.

In the Courts of Heaven, apply Scriptures to your situation, and present them as evidence for your case. Before you enter the court, make sure you have confessed your sins. You will have a clean slate when you present your case. Victory will be your verdict.

If you are attacked by the devil for not forgiving, you might be sick in body, or angry and bitter. You will heal when you go through the steps and pardon those who have wronged you when you forgive yourself.

Tell the Judge, God Almighty, the following in a prayer:

> *Your Honor, I have forgiven those who have wronged me (give Him the list of names and offenses). I remind You of Your promise in Matthew 6:14: "For if you forgive men for their sins, your heavenly Father will also forgive you." Your Word also says, "Let the redeemed of the Lord say so." I hereby declare that the Blood of the Lamb has redeemed me. I ask you to dismiss these demonic claims against me. I ask for complete healing of my body and soul. I ask for a victorious verdict because I belong to Jesus. He gave the final verdict when He was dying on the cross—"It is finished."*

It is now up to us to execute this final verdict. If you speak these instructions on the way to forgiveness, you will be healed. You will walk in love, tall and confident on God's runway. Walking in forgiveness is walking in God's fashion, His way of doing things.

CHAPTER 10
The Ultimate Makeover

"Being confident of this very thing, that He who has begun a good work in you will complete it until the day of Jesus Christ." Philippians 1:6 (NKJV)

Every Friday, I enjoy what I call a "Jeanie-Jean" day. I will either go for a walk on Balboa Island or walk to the beach. I love to get my hair done at a salon, go shopping, or get a facial.

FOUR STEPS TO THE ULTIMATE MAKEOVER

Having an Ultimate Makeover is exciting and makes us feel good about ourselves. There are four major steps to an Ultimate Makeover.

1. Have a Facial

As mentioned in chapter 2, in the natural world, a facial is the first part of a makeover. Cleansing the skin starts the process. Rubbing the product in circles around the face and neck removes facial oils and/or makeup. Let it sit on the skin for a few minutes, and then use a warm, moist towel to remove the cleanser.

Next, exfoliation takes off the dead skin cells, leaving freshly renewed skin. With light pressure, twirl your fingers around the skin to remove the old cells. Sometimes microdermabrasion is used next. This small machine uses diamond chips or crystals for deeper penetration into the skin.

About every eight weeks, you can undergo an anti-aging treatment using glycolic acid. Follow it with a massage of the face and neck for five to ten minutes.

How does this apply to your spiritual life? I have learned to spend time being quiet in God's presence. My body is exfoliated, and all the "dead skin" comes off me. The more I engage with the Holy Spirit, the

---

Knowledge of Jesus and His Word go from my head to my heart.

---

deeper He will penetrate my spirit and soul (mind, will, and emotions). The more knowledge I have of the Bible, the deeper the relationship I have with the Holy Spirit. Knowledge of Jesus and His Word go from my head to my heart.

> *That He (Jesus) might cleanse it (the body) with the washing of water by the Word.*
> —Ephesians 5:26 (KJV)

I spend five minutes to an hour each day reading the Word and praying. Once a week, women come to my home for Bible study and worship. We pray for forty-five minutes to an hour.

As your relationship with Jesus deepens, a greater anointing will exude from your innermost being. When you walk into a room, the atmosphere will change because the light of Christ walks in with you. This will continue to happen as long as you keep that intimate connection with the Holy Spirit. You want to be aligned with His design.

> *But we with unveiled face, beholding as in a mirror the glory of the Lord, are being transformed into the same image from glory to glory, just as by the Spirit of the Lord.*
>
> —2 Corinthians 3:18 (NKJV)

2. Choose Your Clothing

Step 2 of the ultimate makeover applies to the clothes you wear. How do you present yourself on the outside? There are several styles of fashion you can choose from, depending on your taste and/or the occasion. Remember, you can really wear what you want today. Consider your body shape, and look for the style of clothes that fits your look.

For women, categories include trendy, casual, exotic, vibrant, sexy, preppy, elegant, Bohemian, girly, cowgirl, girl next door, punk, artsy, businesswoman, tomboy, Gothic, rocker, fifties, seventies, and sporty.

I will comment on a handful of these.

- "Trendy" encompasses the most up-to-date fashions. For women today, baggy jeans or flared pants with ¾-length coats are fashionable. Accessories can dress up the most boring outfit.

- "Casual" is anything but boring—but it is not flamboyant. It's

116

hard to beat a white T-shirt or sweater with blue jeans and a couple of accessories to go with your outfit for casual, easy-to-manage fashion. Jeans with holes, denim blouses, denim dresses, belts, and blazers all fit into this category. A subcategory of "casual" is "business casual," which includes suits with pants, skirts, and knee-length dresses.

- "Exotic" fashion includes items that most people have not seen before. The more ostentatious the outfit, the better. These clothes are bold and eye-catching, with bright colors. Extreme embroidery is sometimes evident. Add unique jewelry, and you will be noticed from a mile away.

- "Vibrant" is just what it sounds like: bright colors and various patterns that follow a fun and flirty style, such as a flared, flowing skirt that's pink with white flowers.

- "Sexy" relies on trim-fitting skirts and low-cut tops.

- "Preppy" is associated with college students, often including white-collared blouses under pullover sweaters and A-line skirts or leggings.

- "Elegant" usually refers to floor-length evening gowns, although a nice suit can apply as well. Glamorous and classy are the adjectives here.

- "Bohemian" (the "boho" look for short) is comprised of 1960s hippie-type outfits, Think bright, wild patterns with paisley and boots with suede fringe.

Men's fashion does not boast the same broad span of categories. For centuries, men's fashion has been pretty boring. It's either jeans and a T-shirt for casual wear or black/gray/blue business suits with a dress shirt and tie for work and formal occasions.

Today's millennial men in their twenties and thirties are more fashion-oriented. They're willing to experiment with more colors and different designs of jackets and pullovers.

Whereas New York City is the center of women's designer fashion, southern California has become the fashion hub for millennial men. Worldwide, however, Italy—blessed with the exquisite taste of its couturiers—can never be replaced as the top fashion influencer.

Today, men's fashion choices include various labels, called "archetypes." Here are some examples.

- A "Henry" is a high-earning but not-yet-rich kind of guy. He will wear a blazer with pants or a pullover sweater and khakis.

- A "Yummy" refers to the young urban male who will wear an untucked dress shirt over straight-legged jeans, with or without a blazer.

- "The Modern Gent" mixes suits with patterns and textures. The tie and pocket scarf match, along with wing-tip dress shoes and thin, matching shoestrings.

- "The Urban Dapper Dude" wears expensive or trendy sweat-pants.

- The "Upscale Casual Guy" sports an expensive wardrobe with a brightly colored blazer and slacks or a shawl-collar sweater.

- The "Lumbersexual" will wear plaid shirts and sport a well-groomed beard.

- A "Metrosexual" is a heterosexual man with a sensitivity more often seen, stereotypically, in women or gay men. More than most, these men are concerned with their personal appearance. They might wear expensive hairstyles, trimmed beards, form-fitting shirts, and straight-legged jeans.

- "Casual" can refer to hoodies and jeans or T-shirts and shorts.

- "Business casual," again, can mean khaki pants or dark jeans with no holes and either a polo or collared shirt. A blazer over a designer T-shirt looks great with jeans for this look.

- "The Modern Gent" will wear a pinstriped or solid-color suit with a tie and pocket scarf.

- "Formal," of course, includes the tuxedo for eveningwear.[1]

The fashion style you wear expresses your personality. Wearing new clothes is fun. We all need a change from the ordinary. Having a

1. Shan Li. "Millennial Guys Keen on Style Are Reshaping the Fashion Trade," *Los Angeles Times*, March 15, 2015, http://www.latimes.com/business/la-fi-menswear-boom-20150315-story.html.

makeover can be refreshing. As men and women of God, the ultimate makeover is being completely transformed on the inside. Let's dress our hearts with a spirit of excellence. We can look good and be fashionable on the outside without compromising our beliefs.

You don't want to give in to the world's temptations. You live in the world, but you don't have to be degraded by it.

> *Meanwhile we groan, longing to be clothed instead with our heavenly dwelling, because when we are clothed, we will not be found naked.*
> −2 Corinthians 5:2–3 (NIV)

Fashionable clothes aren't just for men and women; teenagers, children, and even babies can wear them. Moms and dads need to teach their children the Word of God so they can learn how to behave. They need to be taught God's instruction and eternal perspective on issues. Children

When they are loved, the young shine with happiness.

thrive with structure, which helps them grow up to be self-confident and feel worthy. When they are loved, the young shine with happiness.

Girls and young women should be taught that life is not about getting hugs and drugs to boost their self-esteem. That is a lie from the pit of hell. When they are taught that they are the children of Almighty God, they will feel loved and highly valued. They need to understand that they are precious. When they are strong and know who they are in Christ, the youth will not give in to peer pressure. They will feel good about themselves and be modest in the way they dress. When they are taught boundaries, they will live by them.

3. Exercise

The third part of the Ultimate Makeover has to do with exercise. I'm not talking about running marathons or pumping heavy weights, but rather regular activity to keep your blood moving. Sports are fun for many people. Just being outside walking, or using a treadmill or elliptical indoors, can lead to good cardiovascular health.

I do Pilates twice a week. I must make an appointment, or it most likely won't get done. I'm busy, like most of us are. I also lift weights, use the elliptical machine, and walk.

Could I do more? Yes, I could. Start with as much as you can handle. Don't think, "Oh my gosh, that's overwhelming." Just take one step at a time.

4. Get the proper nutrition

Getting the proper nutrition is the fourth and final stage of the Ultimate Makeover. "You are what you eat"—you've heard that saying, I'm sure. It's true. If all you eat is fast food, donuts, and pizza, you will not be healthy. Try to eat organic foods, grass-fed meat, and hormone-free dairy products. Again, don't get overwhelmed. Eat more vegetables and fruit, less bread and meat. You don't need to change your diet overnight. Just do what you can.

Pursue your purpose, and desire to know your destiny. You must be healthy so you can accomplish your calling. I encourage you to practice the fruit of the spirit of self-control.

> *What? Do you not now know that your body is the Temple of the Holy Spirit, who is in you, whom you have received from God, and you are not your own?*
> —1 Corinthians 6:19 (MEV)

STRIVE FOR STRONG MENTAL HEALTH, TOO

Healthy bodies are connected to healthy minds. A healthy mind brings healthy thoughts. Healthy thoughts are filled with assurance and trust, which come from your relationship with Jesus Christ. When your spirit spends time daily with the Holy Spirit, your faith grows, as well as your knowledge of who Jesus is in your life.

A flourishing spirit, mind, and body will help you walk the fashion runway with courage and confidence. This is done by focusing your eyes forward, not looking at the crowd. Your chin should be down slightly because the people in the audience are seated and looking up to you. Your shoulders should be back and down and not move much. Women's upper arms should be close to the body so the lower arms can swing a little. Men's arms should swing more fully due to their longer strides. Relax your hands. Make sure they are not curled under.

Fashion modeling is not just for the young. Most older models have taken care of themselves and still exude vitality and vigor in the way they look and walk. Wisdom and life experiences are conveyed by the mature images of the fashion industry. Often, older models will give tips and pointers to the younger generation on what to expect and how to handle various situations.

Mature models of the Kingdom of God are similar. Usually, but not always, they are older in age. People who have studied the Word of God and have applied it to their lives encourage others, young and old. They teach the younger and older generations in the ways of the Lord. Proverbs

Proverbs is the book of wisdom.

is the book of wisdom. It instructs us on how to respond to various circumstances. It suggests boundaries for the wise to apply to our lives. It creates a hunger for the Holy Spirit in those who desire more of God. Strong believers speak the goodness and faithfulness of the Almighty One.

> *Generation after generation will declare more of Your*
> *greatness and declare more of Your glory.*
> Psalm 145:4 (TPT)

Wisdom comes with a sound mind. Mental stability is required for clear thinking. You must concentrate to know how to process the circumstances of your existence. This knowledge is imperative to avoid the pitfalls that can derail your walk with God.

When you have a healthy thought life, your spirit is in control. You have chosen God to have reign over how you think. Romans 12:2 reminds us to "be transformed by the renewing of your mind."

Being *transformed* is a transition in the very nature of your thought process. It is about reflection, not contamination. A well-known preacher describes it like this:

> *You sow a thought; you reap an act.*
> *You sow an act; you reap a habit.*
> *You sow a habit; you reap a character.*
> *You sow a character; you reap a destiny!*

One Sunday afternoon, my husband and I were looking at houses, and I got a call on my cell phone from the company that operates our home security system. The alarm had gone off, and the police had been called to check it out. We were thirty minutes from home, so there was nothing I could do right then. Fear tried to grip me. We had gone to church that morning and heard a message about trusting God, no matter what. I began speaking in tongues and declaring protection over our home.

I kept saying, "Nothing missing, nothing broken." My spirit calmed me down.

But there was no intruder. The day before, we had hosted a birthday party for our oldest son. He was excited to be eleven years old. We had tied balloons together in the living room, and they were blowing around from the wind of the heater. That caused the motion detector to go off the next day, which is why we got the call.

An event such as this can cause our thoughts to spin out of control. But we can maintain control over our thoughts.

MAKE OVER YOUR INTERNAL BEING

The ultimate makeover is being renewed from your face to your feet—being cleansed and dressed on the outside as well as on the inside of your being. The outside includes a facial, massage, and wearing new, fashionable clothes. The inside pertains to cleansing of the heart, good nutrition, exercise, and healthy thoughts. It's not as much about a *makeover* as it is a *takeover*.

CHAPTER 11
Pursuit of Purity

"All who have this hope in Him purify
themselves, just as He is pure."
1 John 3:3 (NIV)

When you walk the runway of God's design, you are in the pursuit of purity.

Purity is a person. Purity is Jesus. He was the Son of God, who became the Son of Man, yet without sin. He is the definition of purity.

Think about holding up a glass full of ice-cold water. It's clear, pure, and tastes oh, so good. This fresh water will taste best after you run around a track or sweat it out on the elliptical or treadmill in the gym. There's nothing like it, right?

Now think of your life. What are you filling your spirit with? Good words? Bad words? Gray words? Do you watch too much TV? News?

What are you filling your spirit with?

Movies? Do you spend a lot of time on social media?

Why would you want to be pure? After all, this is the twenty-first century. Everybody knows that life is all about what feels good, what's right at the moment—because you deserve it, right? People often think, "Hey, everybody is doing it; why not me? I just want to be happy." The world works that way. But this is a narcissistic way of thinking: "Me, me, me. I want what I want, and I want it *now*."

As Christians, we are to have a different mindset. We are to have the mind of Christ—to believe that the way Jesus thinks is revealed to us by the Holy Spirit when we read and study the Word of God with a spiritual hunger for who He is. The passage of Scripture in 1 Corinthians 2:10–16 verifies this truth. That is why we have God's instruction: to show us how to see things according to His understanding. Look at life from an eternal perspective, to see clearly and understand the faith and authority given to you by your relationship with Jesus Christ. Living in a natural frame of reference is normal. However, blessings come from putting our love for Jesus first in our lives. He has so much to show you. Why wouldn't you want to spend time with Him?

> *But seek first the kingdom of God and His righteousness,*
> *and all these things shall be added to you.*
> —Matthew 6:33 (NKJV)

When you make Him your top priority, you can be pure and successful. You can make a difference in the world you live in. You can be a strategic influence in whatever industry you are a part of. You are designed to bring heaven to Earth in these last days.

"Purity" means freedom from anything that contaminates or pollutes; freedom from any mixture or modifying addition; or freedom from guilt or evil (shame).

BE FREE FROM CONTAMINATION

Leviticus 14:33–42 explains this concept. The author talks about how the stones of the tabernacle had become moldy and were spreading filth. The contractors were instructed to take out the contaminated stones. They were to throw them out of the city into a quarantined area. Then they were to replace the contaminated rocks with *fresh stones* and new *clay*.

According to 1 Peter 2:4–5, "You also, like *living stones*, are being built into a spiritual house to be a holy priesthood..."

The Bible compares Christians to clay. Isaiah 4:8 says, "Yet you, LORD, are our Father. We are the *clay*, you are the Potter; we are all the work of your hand." The Potter is the one who shapes his design from the clay. God is the one who shapes your life into His fashion. We allow Him to form our purpose through obedience to His Word.

Hebrews 4:12 (NKJV) says, "The Word of God is living and powerful and sharper than any two-edged sword." That includes the Old Testament. The more you read and study the Word, the fresher the revelation that is given to you. A closer, more intimate relationship with Jesus is the result.

If you are not there yet, don't get down on yourself. Let go of the past, and focus on the future.

*And such WERE some of you. But you were **washed**, but*

*you were **sanctified**, but you were **justified** in the Name of*
the Lord Jesus and by the Spirit of our God.
—1 Corinthians 6:11 (MEV)

The only way to keep the mold—sin—from spreading in your life is to be cleansed with the *elegance of purity*, the Word of God, daily. The river of God in Psalm 1 represents how your soul (mind, will, emotions) and body are cleansed and made pure by the Holy Spirit.

We go from contamination to revelation.

My husband and I often like to relax in the evenings and will click on Netflix looking for a fun comedy, or sometimes a drama or a documentary. I can't tell you how many times we will pick a movie, thinking it will be a good chick flick or PG-13 comedy, only to find someone who is having an affair or committing a murder. Let alone the vulgar language.

Although Hollywood continues to produce morally corrupt movies, we can and should support good movies. Movieguide.org and PureFlix. com are two companies that show pure content.

Let us support the good movies. We are to be the light in the world. How do we do that? By staying away from contamination.

Do not share in the sins of others. Keep yourself pure.
—1 Timothy 5:22b (NIV)

DISCERN AMONG THE MIXTURE OF SPIRITS

Daniel 2:43 says, "And just as you saw the iron mixed with baked clay, so the people will be a *mixture* and will not remain united any

---

There are 41,000 denominations in the world.

---

more than iron mixes with clay." Much *mixture* is in the church today. There are 41,000 denominations in the world.

Talk about mixture. All these denominations believe in God Almighty and that Jesus Christ is the Son of God, but they throw in individual doctrines, which have created the various belief systems.

We must be aware of a *mixture* of spirits among Christians. Learn to discern. Don't let anyone lay hands on you for prayer or offer prophesy to you because they say they "have a Word from God." Listen to the Holy Spirit. Does He want you to hear what they have to say? If something is said and you know it is wrong or you don't feel right about it, bind those words out loud as soon as you realize it. Say something like, "Those words are not God's words. They don't line up with the truth of the Word of God. I break their assignment on my life. I grab hold of those words and say they are null and void in the Name of Jesus."

At a Christian group meeting, my friend was approached by a woman who had a "word" with her. My friend didn't feel at ease about it but listened anyway. A week later, my friend had a dream. She dreamed that she was in the kitchen, and a snake slithered over to where she stood. She grabbed a knife and cut the snake's head off. She immediately woke up. She knew what the woman had said to her was demonic. We must learn to discern the right voices.

Many gatherings are full of *mixture*. As soon as you realize that wrong words have been spoken to you or you have a bad dream, immediately and vocally cancel the assignment from the enemy. Again, be aware and learn to discern.

BE FREE FROM GUILT AND SHAME

Remember, guilt stems from behavior. Shame has to do with how you feel as a person. To get rid of shame, you must become vulnerable. Becoming vulnerable is allowing yourself to become susceptible to emotional injury.

Unfortunately, being vulnerable opens up a person to getting hurt again. But the more you talk about your shame, the less it hurts you. The more you expose the reason for your shame, it will become less and less prominent in your life. You will realize you are not the only person suffering. You will take comfort in knowing you are not alone. You will realize there are many others in the same predicament. When you share what you have gone through with others, they will gain hope that they, too, can be liberated from oppression.

If you need to be set free, pray this prayer. Say it from your heart, not your head.

> *Father God, thank you for giving Your one and only Son to die on the cross for me. I confess that I am a sinner. I can't live life on my own strength. Right now, I ask you Jesus to be Lord of my life. I will love You and serve You forever! In Jesus's name, Amen.*

If you prayed that prayer just now or you are recommitting your life to Jesus, you have made a wonderful decision. You are now 100 percent committed to God, no matter what.

You will feel like the weight of being pushed down has been lifted off you. You will desire to live a clean life. Learning to live a fresh life is a process. Living to be pure is a lifelong journey. Four areas in our lives are key to this purity. The first is our hearts.

BE PURE OF HEART

> *Blessed are the **pure** in heart, for they shall see God.*
> —Matthew 5:8

When you are born again and ask Jesus to be number one in your life, the Holy Spirit comes to live in your spirit. When that happens, you are declared righteous in God's eyes. That means your spirit has become one with the Holy Spirit, who is righteous and pure.

BE PURE IN THOUGHT

The human soul is different from the human spirit. Each of us is a three-part being—a spirit, a soul, and a body. The soul represents our mind, will, and emotions. So, when we were born again, our spirits were born again, but our souls must be reset daily, sometimes even moment by moment.

Ephesians 4:23 (NLT) says, "Instead, let the Spirit *renew* your thoughts and attitudes." We do that by praising God, speaking His Word, and praying in tongues. Renewing your mind refreshes your spirit.

> *Finally, brethren, whatever thing are **true,** whatever things are **noble,** whatever things are **just,** whatever things are **pure,** whatever things are **lovely,** whatever things are of **good report,** if there is any virtue, and if there is anything praiseworthy—meditate **think** on these things.*
> —Philippians 4:8 (NKJV)

Speaking the Word of God controls your thinking and makes your thoughts pure. Vocalize the promises that apply to your circumstances.

It would be nice if we could do this once and all the negative concepts would disappear, but sometimes we must do this repeatedly to get through a situation. Believe God's promises by faith.

Long ago, I know a woman who didn't take hold of her damaging thoughts about her husband, who had harmed her emotionally. She allowed those hurtful thoughts to sink deeper and deeper into her soul. Perhaps she didn't know how to cope with being put down constantly. Continuous negative thoughts have been medically proven to damage the neurons in your brain. Years of mean words went by, and she didn't confront the man she had married. She knew she would be emotionally lambasted again and nothing good would come out of it. She ignored what she should have done. Women typically didn't speak their minds back in those days.

The avoidance resulted in bitterness. She ended up getting breast cancer and dementia. Trauma can change your personality and health. How sad. I encourage you right now to grab your painful thoughts and give them to Jesus. He will heal your emotional heart.

BE PURE IN SPEECH

Our words are important. God created the Earth with His Words. We, too, create our world with our words. Our sphere of influence is dictated by what we vocalize.

Have you ever considered whether you are positive or negative with your words? Do you say "Thank you," or do you complain? Do you praise God and speak words of faith, or do you cuss and spread the lies of the devil?

> *For by your words you will be justified, and by your*
> ***words*** *you will be condemned."*
> —Matthew 12:37 (MEV)

When we don't keep our speech pure, we open the door for the enemy to creep into our minds. When that happens, our thoughts can be corrupted. It is up to us to retrain our thinking to align with good reflections.

KEEP YOUR BODY PURE

> *Jesus said, "The light of the body is the eye. Therefore, if*
> *your eye is clear, your whole body will be full of light."*
> —Matthew 6:22 (MEV)

Our bodies have five senses: sight, hearing, taste, touch, and smell.

Regarding sight, what do you habitually look at? There is power in what your eyes see.

> *I will set no wicked thing before my eyes.*
> *I hate the work of those who turn aside.*
> *It shall not have a part of me.*
> —Psalm 101:3 (MEV)

The Message (MSG) translation says of that verse, "I refuse to take a second look at corrupting people and degrading things. Stay clear of *contamination.*"

Second, what do you usually listen to?

What you hear makes you happy or sad. Personally, rap music and acid rock are offensive to me. I mainly listen to Christian music, either upbeat praise or worship music, which is soft and pensive. We become what we dwell on. I also love classical music, especially chamber music, such as Vivaldi, Bach, and Mozart. I also like to listen to soft jazz.

What you hear makes you happy or sad.

Sometimes I will flip the channels on Sirius radio and listen to the 1940s music of Bing Crosby or Jimmy Dorsey for a change.

Third, what kind of food do you normally eat? How are your taste buds? Do you consume nourishing foods or junk foods? Our bodies are temples of the Holy Spirit. A healthy diet provides us with the energy to do what we have been called to do. In the natural world, what kind of food do you hunger for?

In the supernatural world, let's develop a hunger for the Word, which is Jesus, the Bread of Life, so we can be divinely transformed into His image. Let's be energized by the anointing of the Holy Spirit.

> *Let's make a clean break with everything that defiles or distracts us, **both within and without**. Let's make our entire lives fit and holy temples for the worship of God.*
> —2 Corinthians 7:1 (MSG)

Fourth, regarding touch, learn to have boundaries. Know them before you find yourself in a seemingly compromising position. Be a person of integrity.

Fifth, regarding your sense of smell, desire to have your life exude a pleasant scent.

> *Now thanks be to God who always causes us to triumph in Christ And through us reveals the **fragrance** of His knowledge in every place.*
> —2 Corinthians 2:14 (MEV)

EXAMINE YOUR MORAL ABSOLUTES

Now that you have worked with your physical senses, examine your moral absolutes. What does it mean to be holy? The natural world is not holy—in fact, it's quite the opposite when it comes to morality. Millions of people are influenced by what they see on TV, in the movies, and on social media. If you are in that world, not in the Word, it will be easy to compromise your morals.

Life is full of distractions. When I get up in the morning, I get dressed and eat breakfast. I enjoy using my iPad to read a devotion for the day and then Scripture. After that, I head up to my study and pray. Most days, that's what I do. But sometimes my phone will ring, and I'll answer it. Other times, I will go to the office, and my attention will get diverted, so I'll start doing office work. They are things I need to do but are distractions from prayer.

Priorities are a moment-by-moment issue. Living in purity is a choice.

If we continually choose not to walk in peace and holiness, we will not be close and intimate with the Holy Spirit. We will miss seeing what Jesus is doing. We will miss His plan for our destiny.

When you know the power of the Holy Spirit has been given to you, you can have freedom from contamination, mixture, guilt, and shame. No longer do you need to feel insecure and inadequate. You will be pure in heart. When you are free, you can be released to be the woman or man you are designed to be.

Will you mess up? Of course. Probably often, but when you do, ask forgiveness, get back in line with His design, and focus forward.

When you walk the runway of God's fashion, you will have the power of the Holy Spirit to be a model of purity.

Let no one despise your youth, but be an example to the believers in word, in conduct, in love, in spirit, in faith, in **purity.**

—1 Timothy 4:12 (NKJV)

We enjoy power in purity. Therefore, obedience is power.

The pursuit of purity is ultimately the pursuit of Jesus. I want to be more like Him. I want my story to be for His glory.

CHAPTER 12
Walking the Runway

"For we walk by faith, not by sight."
2 Corinthians 5:7 (NKJV)

Walking is moving. Walking is action. It is doing, not just being. Faith is *not* just about devotion—it's about *motion*. Life is all about walking by faith. By the time you get to the runway, you have taken off the old clothes, been cleansed in the Spa of Heaven, and found your identity. You have dealt with guilt and shame, rejection, abandonment, and forgiveness. You have experienced a breakthrough in your life.

You have gone through the Ultimate Makeover and are now ready to walk the runway of God's design. In the natural world, you need good self-esteem to be a fashion model and walk with a feeling of confidence

You are an ambassador for the Kingdom of God.

when you're representing a designer. So, too, in the supernatural world, you are an ambassador for the Kingdom of God. You are clothed with the glory of God. Therefore, you can walk with assurance and certainty on God's runway.

In modeling, learning to walk is a step-by-step process. You walk heel to toe, one foot in front of the other, with tall posture, head straight forward. Your arms must be relaxed, with minimal movement.

FACIAL EXPRESSIONS REVEAL YOUR INNER BELIEFS

Our facial expressions are quite revealing. They indicate what we're feeling.

In the fashion world, six facial expressions are important. They are often dictated by the clothes being presented. The *natural* look shows peace and contentment. *Someplace else* is a distant look, as if you are a million miles away. *Happy* is the sign of pleasure and satisfaction. The *blank* look is devoid of expression. *Dynamic* has flirty appeal, with a bit of mystery in the eyes. The *junior* look portrays a happy face with a big smile, although it isn't seen often in runway modeling today.[1]

A model for the Kingdom of God should radiate peace and contentment. A natural smile is always welcome to those around you. You must learn a different walk—one that revolves around your manner of life, your character, and your behavior. You can't snap your fingers and move from here to there. This walk takes time.

HAVE A SPIRIT OF OBEDIENCE

In my life, I have walked God's runway pretty straight. I've never been much of a rebel, although I was in the eighth grade—when I wore blue jeans to school every day, despite my mom wanting me to wear a

---

1. "Runway Facial Expressions," Barbizon Insider, http://www.barbizoninsider. com/runway-facial-expressions.

dress. Also, I wanted to get my ears pierced, but my parents frowned on that. Instead of paying to pierce my ears, I pierced them myself.

A few days later, at dinner with my dad, I put my hair behind my left ear, exposing the gold earring. He looked at me and said, "You didn't."

I said, "I did!"

That was the end of the conversation.

There have been other times, too, when I would get out of line with my attitude. For the most part, I am a positive person, but sometimes I must still watch out for negative thoughts.

Now, when I wake up in the morning, I say, "Good morning, Holy Spirit. Good morning, Jesus. Good morning, Abba Father, I am your beloved, and you are mine."

With those words, I like to say that I am 100 percent committed to God, no matter what. Tell God you will walk in His purpose today. Ask for an increased desire to read the Bible so you will know how to walk. Ask for a fresh anointing, a fresh revelation, as you walk in His Word today. Put a smile on your face as you walk tall and confident.

> *When you walk, your steps will not be hindered, and*
> *when you run, you will not stumble.*
> —Proverbs 4:12 (MEV)

BE A MODEL FOR THE KINGDOM OF GOD

In my teens and twenties, I participated in a few fashion shows and walked a runway. It was fun to walk and display an outfit and then rush back behind the stage and change the outfit and rush out there again to represent a designer's fashions.

Despite the rush, I didn't want to go to New York and have that lifestyle. It was too intense and competitive for me. But I did enjoy my experiences. At the time, I was doing something out of the ordinary. Fashion has always been fun for me. Etiquette and modeling school contributed to who I am today.

I encourage you to be a model for the Kingdom of God. Desire to act on what you have learned from reading the Bible. Be known as one who puts God's principles into practice.

> *But be doers of the Word, and not hearers only, deceiving*
> *yourselves.*
> —James 1:22 (NKJV)

A *doer* is a performer. One who *performs* is an entertainer who carries out "an action or pattern of behavior." The pattern of a biblical *doer* is one who acts on what he or she has heard from the Word until it becomes a part of life.

In modeling, I was a performer. I played the role of fashion model. I would walk straight and tall, one foot in front of the other, with a bounce to my step.

How important is it for you to be a model for the Kingdom of God? Desire to portray His fashion, His way of doing things, and to walk in humility. The Scripture in 1 Peter 5 talks about us being "clothed in humility." How do you humble yourself? Verse 7 in the New Living Translation tells us to "give all your worries and cares to God, for He cares about you." When you cast all your anxiety on Jesus, that shows Him you realize you can't take care of those worries on your own. You let go of pride and give all those situations to Him.

Many people today walk in anxiety, mainly because they are busy. They have no time for friends. Isolation becomes the norm.

The majority of people no longer go to church.[2] They work all week and want to relax on the weekends. Because of this fact, you might be the only Jesus who people in your sphere of influence will ever see. You are Jesus's hands to give, His arms to hug, and His feet to walk on God's runway of life.

WALK IN THE WAYS OF GOD

To walk in the ways of God without making a big mistake, you must live daily with a humble heart of repentance, forgiveness, and obedience to the Word of God. You must walk in integrity. Commit to this

---

2. "The State of the Church 2016," Barna.com, https://www.barna.com/research/state-church-2016.

type of walk:

W—Wisdom

A—Anointing

L—Love

K—Keys

- **Wisdom**—"Jesus has been made unto me wisdom..." (1 Cor. 1:30). When you have the Holy Spirit dwelling in your heart, you have the spirit of wisdom residing in your innermost being. When you need it, just ask.

If any of you lack wisdom, let him ask of God who gives to all men liberally and without criticism, and it will be given to him.
—James 1:5 (MEV)

- **Anointing**—In the Bible, the anointing is represented by the oil of the Holy Spirit being put on God's people for consecration and sanctification. The Holy Spirit living inside of us causes us to be anointed and full of His presence.

But you have an anointing from the Holy One, and you know all things.
—1 John 2:20 (MEV)

- **Love**—This is the deepest, strongest affection known to mankind. God *is* love. We can love because God first loved us. The Holy Spirit dwelling in you causes you to love others who might not be so lovable.

  And now these three remain: faith, hope and love. But the greatest of these is love.
  —1 Corinthians 13:13 (NIV)

- **Keys**—These are keys of the Kingdom of God that represent secrets and weapons that Christians have for their use at any time. Today, Christians need to be taught these secrets and weapons so they can use them wisely.

  *Jesus said, "And I will give you the **keys** of the kingdom of heaven, and whatever you bind on earth will be bound in heaven, and whatever you loose on earth will be loosed in heaven."*
  —Matthew 16:19 (NKJV)

WALK THE WORD BY FAITH

Praise, worship, prayer, giving, and walking in obedience are some of the secret weapons we have access to when we walk boldly to the throne of grace. Of course, walking the Word by faith is a huge key.

When you walk by faith, you advance in the keys of the kingdom that are already inside you. Not only do you learn to *walk* by faith, you learn to *speak* by faith.

Remember, the words you speak are important. There is power in your words. If all that you say is negative—"I'm sick and tired of this situation"—your body will eventually become sick and tired. But if you express positive words—"I'm blessed and highly favored"—then that is what you will be. Don't waste your words and say, "I didn't really mean that."

If you say something, you will believe it. If someone else says something to you, maybe you will hear it, and maybe not. You have an inner voice—your conscience. When you are born again, the Holy Spirit is the still, small voice. You have a choice to listen to Him or ignore Him.

You have an inner voice—
your conscience.

But speaking those words out loud reinforces what you hear inside you. Your words have the power to dictate the atmosphere that surrounds you.

Death and life are in the power of the tongue, and those
who love it will eat its fruit.

—Proverbs 18:21 (NKJV)

Jesus said,

> *For by your words you will be justified, and by your*
> *words you will be condemned.*
> —Matthew 12:37 (NKJV)

Confession is possession. You will have what you say. When you speak the promises of God and believe them, you will see them come to pass. Deuteronomy 28 is the Bible chapter on blessings for obedience. Declare those verses, and put your name in there. Proclamation becomes ownership.

No one else on the face of this planet has the voice you have. Science has proven that your vocal chords contain certain sound waves from vibrating air molecules that are unique to your voice. Many variables cause you to have your particular voice. This includes the structure and size of your bones, eardrum, body, and vocal chords.

Speaking the Word of God causes the Lord to hear His promises and the angels to be released to execute them.

> *Are not all angels ministering spirits sent to serve those*
> *who will inherit salvation?*
> —Hebrews 1:14 (NKJV)

YOUR WORDS AND ACTIONS SHOW WHO YOU ARE

Your words expose what you are thinking—what you dwell on. "As a man thinks, so is he" (Prov. 23:7). Your words then become your manner of life—how you walk. What you say is what you will do.

Since I was a baby—in fact, when I was in my mother's womb—I would go to church every Sunday morning and evening and Wednesday nights as well. I didn't know it then, but people would watch us. Our neighbors saw my family all dressed up, getting in the car and going to church every Sunday.

Whether you realize it or not, people know what you do, where you go, and how you respond to others. Are you kind and considerate? Do you smile? Do you make wise decisions? Not only do your neighbors watch; people at work watch you. People at church watch you. And today on social media, people watch you there, too.

> *Let us walk properly, as in the day, not revelry and*
> *drunkenness, not in lewdness and lust, not in strife and*
> *envy.*
> —Romans 13:13 (NKJV)

Walk in the purpose God has fashioned you for. Walk worthy of your calling. Walk according to the Word. Walk the runway of God's design. Walk in boldness and confidence. Walk in integrity, not intimidation.

CHAPTER 13
Release and Reward

"Commit your way to the Lord; trust in Him and He will do this: He will make your righteous reward shine like the dawn..."
Psalm 37:5–6 (NIV)

When fashion models have completed a show, they often congregate in a special banquet room and celebrate the successful program. They pat each other on the back and say, "Great job! You were fabulous."

Perhaps a few will be rewarded with the designer clothes they wore on the runway.

God will reward us by releasing us into our destiny. We will wear our Designer's label—the glory of God—which is the outward expression of who He is. His presence emanates in light. Jesus is the Light of the World. The Light of the Holy Spirit shines on our human spirits and then exudes from our innermost being. Glory is emanating. God will use your unique personality to display His glory.

LIVE WITH A SPIRIT OF VICTORIOUS VIRTUE

Everyone is different. We all have distinct characteristics. We might look, sound, or act similar, but there is no one on the planet exactly like us. We are fashioned in God's DNA—Divine Nature Anointing.

We are fashioned in God's DNA—Divine Nature Anointing.

With God's DNA inside, I encourage you to run your life with a spirit of victorious virtue. Chase after the knowledge of who you were created to become. Be 100 percent committed to Jesus Christ. He will reward you with increased glory. Glory grows just as love intensifies. God is love. The more you know a friend, the greater your love is for him or her. With the Holy Spirit living inside you, the eyes of your heart are open to what He has planned for your life. Desire your destiny, which is what God has written in your book in Heaven, the Lamb's Book of Life. (See Revelation 21:27.)

> *But without faith it is impossible to please Him, for he*
> *who comes to God must believe that He is, and that He is*
> *a **rewarder** of those who diligently seek Him.*
> —Hebrews 11:6 (NKJV)

PLAN, PREPARE, AND ALLOW TIME FOR THE PROCESS

The reward is not immediate. Life is a process. We are in preparation to be released at the appropriate time. God alone knows the timing. Expect it to come.

In anticipation of a fashion show that's about to start, models are all dressed and standing in the right order to walk the runway and show off a designer's fashions. One at a time, models walk the runway and display the artistic talent of the designer. All the months of planning and preparing have come to a defining moment.

Similarly, we are to plan and prepare to walk the runway God has made for each of us. We plan by thinking, imagining, and writing down ideas for life, business, and ministry. Always have a journal with you so you can record the thoughts that come to mind.

Be alert. Anticipate those valuable nuggets of information when the Holy Spirt downloads them into your heart. Expect creative ideas to make your life a platform of the extraordinary.

Getting to the stage where you will walk your supernatural runway of God's design includes daily and vocally putting on the full armor of God, as discussed in Ephesians 6. Examples of what to say (Declarations) are at the end of this book.

ALWAYS BE READY TO SHARE THE BLESSINGS OF PEACE WITH OTHERS

As mentioned in chapter 7, part of the armor of God includes the shoes you wear. Shoes have many styles and functions. Sneakers are made for running. Flats or loafers accompany casual wear. Sandals are for casual occasions and hot days. For nice occasions, men wear dress shoes, and women wear pumps or high heels.

In the supernatural world, you will want to wear "shoes" that will enable you to "always be ready to share the blessings of peace." (See

Ephesians 6:15, TPT.) Jesus is peace. Imagine slipping into Jesus's shoes. We are already clothed with His presence in the garments of salvation and the robes of righteousness. Why not wear His shoes and be prepared to walk with the Word in your heart? When the Holy Spirit prompts us, we should share the love of Jesus and the Good News wherever we go.

Talking about what God has done in your life is your *testimony*—your story of what you have experienced. No one can deny what you have gone through. Your life experiences are unique. I have a friend who takes Christian students to college campuses to share their two-minute stories of what Jesus has done for them. They meet students on campus and in athletic departments. They build relationships through conversation. Then they tell them their personal accounts of how they heard of Jesus and amazing miracles they have experienced. When my friend and the group have finished sharing, they ask the students if they would like to accept Christ as their Savior. If the students say yes, they say a prayer to ask Jesus to enter their lives and ask for forgiveness of their sins. The Holy Spirit comes to dwell in their spirits, and they are born again.

Many lives have been changed by the power of the Holy Spirit, as evidenced in the love of Jesus that these storytellers describe.

GOD'S HEALING POWER IS REAL

I have traveled the world with ministries that share the love of Jesus. Talking about the healing that Jesus did while He was on Earth causes faith to increase. Those who believe expect to be healed. Many times, a speaker asks people with back pain to stand. The believers in the audience stretch out their hands in the prayer of agreement toward a person standing. The person who has spoken prays for resurrection power to flow through the ones believing for his or her healing.

After the prayer, the person checks to see if he or she still has back pain or feels better. Those with no more pain often rush the stage or to the front to share their good news.

When people are shown God's love by being healed, they want to *know* the Holy Spirit, not just *know about* Him.

During one trip, I witnessed a woman with leukemia. She was determined to get healed. Her face was gray and sad. The pastor prayed over her as the rest of the people prayed in tongues. Her breakthrough came quickly. Her face lit up in a huge smile. The color came back to her face. The glory of God was all over her. She was released from her anguish. She went to the doctor that following week. He ran tests and confirmed that not a trace of leukemia was left in her body.

In 2011, I was in Albania. I was traveling with Marilyn Hickey and a group of ministering tourists. We were meeting in a large gymnasium. In the back of the gym, a mom was holding her son's hand. He was about eight years old. He was deaf in both ears. Sarah Bowling, who is Marilyn's daughter, went over and talked to the mom. Sarah prayed, put her hands on the boy's ears, and commanded the Eustachian tubes to open in the Name of Jesus. Oh, my goodness, they opened instantly! The boy's eyes got really big. He pointed to his ears. He made sounds with his voice, but of course, he couldn't talk yet. He had been deaf since birth.

I have been in gatherings where people were healed of cancer. In December 2017, I was at a meeting in which the pastor called out a woman with cancer. The audience prayed for her while the pastor ministered to her. After a short amount of time, she pressed on her stomach. The pain was gone.

DECLARE VICTORY OVER ILLNESS

People need to be taught how to keep their healing. Many times, people will go back to their familiar surroundings, and the symptoms will return. The person then might say, "Oh, I guess those prayers didn't work on me." That is the wrong thing to say. You must stay around people of faith, speak those promises of healing, and remove the doubt.

I suffered a neck injury when I was sixteen years old. After that, I had endured a loud ringing in my left ear. In a gathering like the one above, the speaker asked those with ringing ears to stand and be healed. I stood.

Those around me prayed out loud that those ringing symptoms would disappear in the name of Jesus. Immediately, the ringing stopped.

Later that night, back in the hotel room, my ear started to ring again. I said out loud, "Oh, no, you don't! I was healed this evening. Now, symptoms, go!" They did.

The disorder tried to come back several more times, and I would say the same thing. "On [*the date it happened*], I was healed in my ear. Now, go!" After a few days, the signs stopped recurring. That was five years ago.

Watch your words, and declare vocally that you were healed on a certain date. Stand in faith.

Numerous times, I have heard about various symptoms of cancer disappearing. The pain disappeared. Lumps vanished. I have seen before and after X-rays that show complete healing.

Seeing people getting healed is wonderful. Talk about being released! Released from pain, disease, misery, and bondage.

As fashion models of the Ultimate Designer, we are to learn to heal the sick. It is not hard to do. When you believe you have the faith and authority to pray God's Word, the Holy Spirit takes over and does the healing. The name of Jesus is what heals. We just need to be bold and believe.

They will lay hands on the sick, and they will recover.

—Mark 16:18b (NKJV)

That is how we walk the runway of God's design. We walk by faith. We claim promises from the Word of God. We shine God's presence wherever we go throughout the day.

Arise, Shine; for your light has come! And the glory of the
LORD is risen upon you.
—Isaiah 60:1 (NKJV)

To shine is to reflect light. To shine is to radiate the brightness of the source. In the natural world, the light comes from the sun. In the supernatural world, the light comes from the Son.

This is the time to step out of your comfort zone. This is the time to be a shining light, unhindered by darkness.

We are released at this time. Let's not get weary in well doing. (See Galatians 6:9, KJV.) Again, preparation is a process. It often takes longer than we think it will. Don't be in a hurry. It is God's timing. Remember, it is a daily, step-by-step walk.

Your runway becomes the place where you run the race so you can receive the crown of Glory. You will be rewarded for walking God's runway by faith, tall with assurance and surety, as well as in humility and meekness.

And whatever you do, do it heartily, as to the Lord And
not to men, knowing that from the Lord you will Receive

*the **reward** of the inheritance; for you serve the Lord Christ.*

—Colossians 3:23–24 (NKJV)

BE RELEASED FROM CARE, SUFFERING, AND ANXIETY

Another way of being released is to be relieved of care or suffering. Release is letting go of anxieties to have the freedom to explore your purpose. Stop procrastinating. Stop holding on to the past. The events you go through in life are intended to prepare you for the reason God has you on this Earth. Peace in your spirit will show you the right thing to do. The closer you get to the Holy Spirit, the more you will understand His reason for making you the way you are.

There are some people only you can reach with God's love. Dr. Charles Stanley said, "This is why He calls believers to positions that have the potential to stretch, mature, and transform them into the people He wants them to be."[1]

Release comes through repentance. Release comes through being faithful and obedient. Freedom is the result. We are released into our purpose. We can set others free from bondage.

Many people are hurting. Broken families. Broken relationships.

1. Dr. Charles Stanley, "God's Purpose for Your Life," In Touch Ministries, March 18, 2015, www.intouch.org/read/Gods-purpose-for-your-life.

Broken people. They need to be loved and told Jesus loves them so much. He gave His life on the cross for them to have hope. That is what they want. That is what they need. You are the one to tell them.

Preparation is a process that comes before promotion. *Promotion* is when we go to the next level of responsibility. Seven "mountains" of career influence our culture, or seven major types of endeavor. They

---

Release comes through repentance.

---

are arts/entertainment, business/economics, education, family, government/law, media, and religion/faith.[2] We are to become leaders at the tops of those mountains in our spheres of influence, our callings.

We are to lead by example, to be models of the Kingdom of God. As we make time with God a priority, this activity gets us ready to walk the runway that God has fashioned for us to walk. Let us have passion for God's fashion.

---

2. Lance Wallnau, "Discover 7M," www.lancewallnau.com/7m-strategy/discover-7m.

EPILOGUE

Now that you have read this book, what will you to do with all this information? How will you learn to walk the runway of God's design? Here are my suggestions.

- Reread the book using a highlighter. Write dates beside the points where you have made decisions to improve your life. This leaves a mark and marks a memorial.

- Get a journal if you don't already have one. Write down the things the Holy Spirit shows you in the Bible. Fresh revelations must be remembered. If you don't write them down, you will probably forget them. I know that happens to me.

- Find a local, faith-based, Bible-believing congregation to call your home church. Locate a church that believes in praising God. Find a group that allows the Holy Spirit to move as He will. A local pastor is a divine covering and a spiritual umbrella. It is important to have a God-given mantle. Psalm 91 talks about resting under that shadow of the Almighty. Being in God's presence is the most secure place to be.

- Get involved in a small Bible study, life group, or small group. Connect with other Christian believers in your community. Being alone is not healthy. You were meant to have conversation, comfort, and encouragement from other Christ followers who are also walking the runway of God's design. They know their God-given purpose and are living it in their daily lives.

If this book has helped encourage you and make your life better, please pass it on to someone who will benefit from the knowledge of being made in the fashion of God's image.

WHO I AM IN CHRIST

I am a chosen generation—1 Peter 2:9

I am royalty—1 Peter 2:9

I am an heir—Galatians 3:29; Colossians 3:24

I am a citizen of heaven—Ephesians 2:19, Philippians 1:27 (NLT)

I am a child of Jesus Christ—Romans 1:5–6

I am not ashamed of the Gospel of Christ for it is the power unto me—Romans 1:16

I am in right standing with God—Acts 10:35

I am sanctified—1 Corinthians 6:11, Hebrews 2:11

I am buried with Him through baptism unto death…walk in newness of life—Romans 6:4

I am dead to sin and alive to God—Romans 6:8 (MSG)

I am a joint heir with Jesus Christ—Romans 8:17

I am in Christ. Therefore I have wisdom, righteousness, sanctification, and redemption—1 Corinthians 1:30

I am a new creation—2 Corinthians 5:17

I am enriched in full power—Micah 3:8a

I am His workmanship created in Christ Jesus—Ephesians 2:10

I am the salt of the Earth—Matthew 5:13

I am the light of the world—Luke 11:36

I am a follower of Jesus Christ—Matthew 10:22

I am forgiven—Mark 2:5

I am blessed because I believe that the Lord will do as He says—Luke 1:45

I am complete—Ephesians 1:23, 3:19, 4:13; James 1:4

I am valuable—Luke 12:24

I am healed—Luke 13:1

I am faithful in little, I will be faithful in much—Luke 16:10

I am born again—John 3:3

I am a friend of Jesus—John 15:15

I am in one spirit with the God head—John 17:23, Romans 7:4, Galatians 3:28

I am God's temple—1 Corinthians 3:17

I am a living stone—1 Peter 2:5

I am healthy in body as my soul prospers—3 John 1:2 (NLT)

I am a friend of Jesus—John 15:15

PUTTING ON THE
FULL ARMOR OF GOD
EPHESIANS 6

- Right now I put on the full armor of God for I know that I don't wrestle against flesh and blood, but against principalities, powers of the air, rulers of darkness, and spiritual wickedness in high places. So I stand and I put on the armor of righteousness (2 Corin. 6:7).

- I put on the belt of truth. And I tighten it. Your Word is Truth (John 17:17). "Jesus is Truth, He said, I **am** the way, the Truth..." It is the foundation of who I am. Therefore, righteousness is my belt and faithfulness the sash around my waist (Isa. 11:5).

- I put on the breastplate of righteousness because I am in right standing with God. Righteousness is a gift (Rom. 5:17). Righteousness comes through grace (Gal. 2:21). I am saved by grace, and Your grace is sufficient. Your Word says, he who practices righteousness is righteous, just as He is righteous (1 John 3:7). So today, I present my body as an instrument of righteousness (Rom. 6:13).

- The glory of the LORD is my rear guard (Isa. 58:8). Jesus is the glory of my strength (Ps. 89:17). The joy of the LORD is my strength. I can do all things through Christ—The Anointed

One and His anointing—Who gives me strength. Today, I am strengthened with might in my inner being (Eph. 3:16).

- I put on the shoes of the gospel of peace so that where I walk, I walk in peace. Those shoes are army boots of Almighty God so I can walk in peace and authority. I walk with the Good News. I walk in love. I walk in wisdom (Col. 4:5). I walk by faith not by sight (2 Corin. 5:7). I walk in the Light and He is in the Light (1 John 1:7). I walk in the Light of His countenance (Ps. 89:15). For His Word is the Lamp unto my feet and the Light unto my path (Ps. 119:105). I walk worthy of my calling (Eph. 4:1). That calling that is irrevocable (Rom. 11:29). Therefore, I walk in the Spirit and do not fulfill the desires of the flesh (Gal. 5:16). I walk in good works, for I was created to walk in them (Eph. 2:10). I no longer walk as the rest of the world in the futility and useless- ness of their minds (Eph. 4:17). Instead, I run the race that is set before me. I focus forward on the prize of that upward calling. I accomplish today what God has called for me to do.

- I put on the helmet of salvation to protect my mind, will, and emotions. This gives me healing, deliverance, and soundness of mind. For I have the mind of Christ.

- Above all, I hold up the shield of faith to "quench (douse, extin- guish) **all** the fiery darts—the flaming missiles of the wicked." My shield is saturated by the Holy Spirit because I am an oak of righteousness planted by the rivers of living water that brings forth fruit in its season (Ps. 1).

- I have the sword of the Spirit, which is the Word of God. The Word is that double-edged sword that goes in my heart and comes out my mouth so that I can pray with all kinds of prayer with perseverance and watchfulness for all believers and say what needs to be prayed for at the right time.

- Today, I have boldness of speech, doors of utterance. I have doors of influence; doors of opportunity because Jesus is the Open Door. I live under an open Heaven. I speak to the right person at the right time and the right way. I speak words that bring life. I speak words of grace seasoned with salt (Col. 4:6). I speak words of faith and edification. I speak words of encouragement. Therefore, my words are seeds of righteousness being planted wherever I go.

WALKING DECLARATIONS

Today, I choose to walk under the cloud of glory. (Rom. 6:4)

I refuse to walk under the cloud of gloom. (1 John 1:6)

I walk by faith, not by sight. (2 Corin. 5:7)

I walk in wisdom. (Col. 4:5)

I walk in the Light as He is in the Light, because God's Word is a lamp unto my feet and a light unto my path. (1 John 1:7, Ps. 119:105)

I walk the paths of righteousness for His Name's sake. (Ps. 23:3)

I walk in peace. (Gal. 6:16, Eph. 6:15)

I walk in joy. (Luke 6:3)

I walk in truth. Jesus is Truth. (3 John 1:4, John 14:6)

Thank you, Holy Spirit, for walking with me today.

IF YOU'RE A FAN OF THIS BOOK, WILL YOU HELP ME SPREAD THE WORD?

There are several ways you can help me get the word out about the message of this book...

- Post a 5-Star review on Amazon.

- Write about the book on Facebook, Twitter, Instagram – any social media you regularly use!

- If you blog, consider referencing the book, or publishing an excerpt from the book with a link back to my website. You have my permission to do this as long as you provide proper credit and backlinks.

- Recommend the book to friends—word-of-mouth is still the most effective form of advertising.

- Purchase additional copies to give away as gifts. You can do that by going to my website at jeanmetcalf.org

The best way to connect with me is at jeanmetcalf.org

China–spoke at woman's conference.

Fiji-spoke at church service.